X.media.publishing

T0223404

Serge Linckels • Christoph Meinel

E-Librarian Service

User-Friendly Semantic Search in Digital Libraries

 Springer

Serge Linckels
Hasso-Plattner-Institut (HPI)
Prof.-Dr.-Helmert-Str. 2-3
14482 Potsdam
Germany
linckels@hpi.uni-potsdam.de

Christoph Meinel
Hasso-Plattner-Institut für
Softwaresystemtechnik GmbH
Prof.-Dr.-Helmert-Str. 2-3
14482 Potsdam
Germany
meinel@hpi.uni-potsdam.de

ISSN 1612-1449
ISBN 978-3-642-26775-8   ISBN 978-3-642-17743-9 (eBook)
DOI 10.1007/978-3-642-17743-9
Springer Heidelberg Dordrecht London New York

Cover design: KünkelLopka GmbH

Printed on acid-free paper

Springer is part of Springer Science+Business Media (www.springer.com)

for Magali, Mathilde, Paul, and Mike
from Serge

for Ivanka, Julia, and Martin
from Christoph

Preface

The key to understanding the breathtaking development of mankind lies in the ability to objectify knowledge. Just like human knowledge has undergone changes, so have the libraries in their role as treasure chambers of said knowledge. With the advent of the digital age, traditional libraries were complemented by huge collections of digital documents. These digital libraries, or e-libraries, result from the fact that knowledge can nowadays be objectified in the form of multifaceted digital copies. Relatively speaking, we are still at the dawn of the digital age—let us not forget that the Web is only three decades old—and yet, the documents that have been collected in a digital library display an astonishing range in terms of multimedia feature diversity: traditional texts, photos, and graphics, recorded audio files (e.g., conversations, music, and sounds of all kinds), moving images (e.g. video sequences, films, or live recordings of events), to name but a few. Future developments will certainly lead to further forms and formats; it is therefore safe to say that the portfolio of digital documents will increase exponentially, and so will the number of digital libraries, consequentially.

As a result of this development, modern users are confronted with new challenges that come in the form of explosions of objectified knowledge caused by digital technology. How does one manage to find the most relevant documents about a certain topic? Who is going to assist the user with this procedure? In traditional libraries of the pre-digital era, one could address the librarian and ask for human assistance. The librarian knew the order by which the book inventory was arranged and could thus give the required information without being an expert on any of the subject matters. When looking for a similar kind of support when using a digital library, one finds first and foremost high-performance keyword search engines, mostly Google, which, despite their considerable capabilities, exhibit limitations when it comes to interacting with the user; their user interfaces have generally not been optimized for this particular task, and they usually suffer from an inability to put the user's query into a precise context.

When using such a search engine, one has to enter individual keywords and then obtains a list of digital documents as a result. These documents have previously been indexed by the search engine and have been marked as highly relevant to the query, merely due to the high occurrence of input keywords. In contrast to the assistance offered by a librarian in former times, one has to rely on the mere use of keywords, knowing that a search engine cannot differentiate between the literal meaning of a keyword and the context respectively subtext of that search item. This book examines the question whether this has to be accepted as a given fact. It describes a vision and identifies ways to develop an electronic service—the E-Librarian Service—that provides users of digital libraries with the service they are accustomed to from a time when they were dealing with a traditional librarian.

To design such an E-Librarian Service, three key components are required. Firstly, an E-Librarian Service needs to "understand" the meaning behind user needs on top of the actual meaning of the search item. In this field, there are several emerging technologies regrouped under the term "Semantic Web and Ontologies" which have the potential to develop into one of the key technologies of the 21st century. These technologies are able to give the users a feel for the importance and semantic meaning of the documents of a digital library and, at the same time, convey the message that the supporting technical systems actually "understand" their needs.

Secondly, efficient technologies are needed so that an E-Librarian Service will be able to provide the most relevant documents systematically for a search topic. The currently developing "Multimedia Information Retrieval" systems give cause for hope that it will be possible to find documents efficiently and reliably, even in digital libraries that largely exceed actual libraries in size and capacity.

Lastly, the users need a human-friendly interface for digital libraries in order to be able to enter their queries in a natural language, i.e., a language they are accustomed to as opposed to an artificial computer language. In fact, there are currently developments in the field of information technologies that make it seem realistic that natural language questions can be processed and "understood" properly by an IT system. The required technologies are referred to as "Natural Language Processing" and "Description Logics and Reasoning".

As a matter of fact, the first implementations of such E-Librarian Services are already being used. As part of his Ph.D. thesis, one of the authors of this book, Serge Linckels, developed an E-Librarian Service called CHESt which high-school students can use to explore knowledge in the field of computer history. CHESt is able to find a clip or several clips that correspond to the queries, in this case complete questions in German or English. The underlying foundation is a digital library that consists of more than 300 video clips that were taped with the tele-TASK system that was developed by Christoph Meinel, who is this book's second author, and his team. Research has proven that CHESt was able to retrieve videos more accurately and precisely than the use of pure keyword search engines would have been able to do. Apart from CHESt, other E-Librarian Services have been developed and tested, such as MatES and the Lecture Butler, and despite the fact that the underlying concepts might remind us of science fiction films, research in this field shows that those E-Librarian Services could eventually become reality.

However, before we introduce the basic ideas regarding the concept and structure of E-Librarian Services and their first implementations, such as CHESt, MatES, or Lecture Butler, we are going to introduce the reader to the underlying technologies, such as "Semantic Web and Ontologies", "Description Logics and Reasoning", "Natural Language Processing" and "Information Retrieval", which are of great interest in themselves. All these technologies have the potential of becoming key technologies of the 21st century and will be dealt with in individual chapters. We greatly enjoyed discovering how these technologies that are currently being developed independently from each other can be combined to create unexpected new possibilities to design services and thus provide new and astonishing results through their application. We hope that the interested reader will share the fun we had and perhaps feel inspired to become creative, too.

We would like to thank the staff of the chair "Internet Technologies and Systems" of the Hasso-Plattner-Institute in Potsdam for their contributions to this book. We would also like to thank Michel Bintener and Sabine Lang for editing, and everybody else who contributed to this book with their comments, suggestions, and reviews.

Serge Linckels and Christoph Meinel
Steinfort/Potsdam, April, 2011

Contents

Part III Applications

Part IV Appendix

1

Introduction to E-Librarian Services

Throughout history, libraries have always been the carriers of knowledge and the instruments for learning from the experiences and endeavors of previous generations. More recently, digital libraries have removed the physical walls of classical libraries by making accessible tremendous amounts of knowledge in multimedia form via a broad variety of electronic tools.

This evolution of libraries confronts modern information retrieval (IR) systems with new challenges. The content in such digital repositories is getting increasingly more complex to process, as it adds multimedia content, such as audio and video documents, to its previously exclusively text-based content. This in turn renders the search of information inside digital libraries increasingly difficult.

Parallel to the changes of content, the expectations and demands which users have towards IR systems are becoming more ambitious. Users expect simple interfaces for optimized and powerful search engines which are able to find the exact answers to their questions.

1.1 From Ancient to Digital Libraries

The collection of written knowledge in some sort of repository is a practice as old as civilization itself [KK01]. About 30,000 clay tablets found in ancient Mesopotamia date back more than 5,000 years. Archeologists have uncovered papyrus scrolls from 1300 – 1200 BCE in the ancient Egyptian cities of Amarna and Thebes, and thousands of clay tablets in the palace of King Sennacherib, an Assyrian ruler from 704 – 681 BCE at Nineveh, his capital city. The name for the repository eventually became *library*, which, in Greek, refers to "a collection of books". The Latin word for *library* is *bibliotheca*.

Early collections of papyri, usually considered as archives rather than libraries, may have surfaced from the Near East, but the ancient Greeks propelled the idea through their heightened interest in literacy and intellectual

Fig. 1.1. Artistic Rendering of "The Great Library of Alexandria" by O. Von Corven.

life. Public and private libraries flourished through a well-established process: authors wrote on a variety of subjects, *scriptoria* produced the books, and book dealers sold them. Copying books was an exacting business in high demand.

The early word for book was *codex* (Latin for: block of wood), which was a Roman invention that replaced the *scroll*. A codex is a book in the format used for modern paper-based books, with separate pages normally bound together inside a cover.

Throughout the 1600s and 1700s, libraries surged in popularity. They grew as universities developed and as national state-supported collections began to appear.

The 20th century saw the continued development of the library through education and organization. Libraries in educational institutions have developed a wide range of services to meet the educational objectives of their parent institutions. School libraries clearly need to support the curriculum, but they also collect books and other materials to encourage reading and inquisitive thinking, as well as to meet the needs of the teachers and administrative staff.

Libraries started to change with the appearance of microfilms in the 1930s and the development of early electronic databases in the 1950s [MS09]. The library profession was becoming increasingly technical.

The growth in electronic media available to the general public and its ease of use have been the catalysts for librarians to adapt to the new information landscape, to develop new services, and to improve library provision. The term *digital library* was first made popular by the NSF-DARPA-NASA Digital Libraries Initiative in 1993.

In the 1990s, large-scale projects were initiated that aimed to digitize and preserve books and other paper-based documents. Improvements in optical character recognition (OCR) and new standards in electronic book formats led to initiatives like Google Books[1], Universal Digital Library[2], Project Gutenberg[3], and Internet Archive[4].

In the past few years, we have been able to witness a tremendous increase in the availability of information throughout knowledge repositories in digital form. For example, at the Hasso-Plattner-Institut (HPI) in Potsdam, Germany, over 30 hours of university lecture videos about computer science are produced every week and added to its archive, which has nearly 10,000 hours of archived lecture material. Most of it is published at the online tele-TASK archive[5].

More recently, novel forms of digital libraries have been developed and intro-duced to a wide audience on the World Wide Web (WWW), e.g., wikis, weblogs, social networks, and file sharing services. Although these types of libraries have unconventional and sometimes chaotic approaches to authoring and organizing content, they manage to attract millions of users every day. Some of these libraries are self-organizing systems where both content and structure are defined by the individuals of the community. This means that ordinary users get involved in the content creation process that was previously mostly restricted to professional information providers. The natural development of library system has thus led to a democratization of the knowledge building and archiving processes.

---

[1] http://www.gutenberg.org/
[2] http://www.ulib.org/
[3] http://www.gutenberg.org/
[4] http://www.archive.org/
[5] http://www.tele-task.de/

1.2 From Searching to Finding

1.2.1 Searching the Web

Web search engines have changed the way people are looking for information. Today, searching for information often means using the WWW by *googling* keywords and browsing through the first page of the results list.

How did people look for information before there was Google, Yahoo!, or even the WWW? People went to libraries and asked the librarian for assistance, or they just walked along the shelves and browsed for books which matched some information they had, like the name of an author, a title, a genre, or some other information about a document, such as the color of the cover or the year of publication.

The librarian or the customer had the possibility to use a register of library cards, which contained information about each document (see figure 1.2)[6]. Generally, a *controlled vocabulary* was used for the description of the documents, e.g., title, author, year of publication, ISBN, type of document, editor, and number of pages. This supplementary information is called *metadata*, i.e., data about data. Most important was a reference or identifier where to find the document in the library.

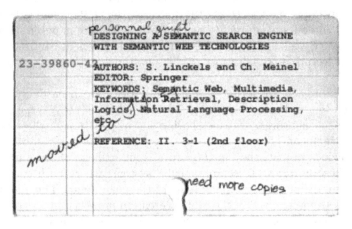

Fig. 1.2. Library card with metadata about a document.

Computer-assisted search of information started in the 1960s with the adoption of database management systems and applications. Classical IR is based on a repository of indexed documents and information needs from a user. The latter are translated into database queries. Different models were created to find best matching documents, e.g., Boolean model or vector space model (see chapter 5).

---

[6] Image created at: http://www.blyberg.net/card-generator/

The WWW can be perceived as an enormous distributed multimedia database with billions of *hypertext* documents. The WWW uses *hyperlinks* as supplementary help for the navigation. The first Web search engine was *Aliweb*, which appeared in 1993 and still runs today [Kos94].

First generation search engines (1995 – 1997) used almost exclusively on-page data such as text and formatting information to compute and rank the answer set. Second generation search engines (since 1998) like Google use off-page, Web-related data, such as link analysis, anchor-texts, and click-through data. The third generation of search engines (since 2003) try to blend data from multiple, heterogeneous sources, trying to answer "the need behind the query". The computed results are customized according to the user's needs and take into account the user's personal data background, context, and intention. They include social networking information, tagging, user feedback, semantic analysis, recommendations, and trustworthiness of information.

Similar to classical IR systems, Web search engines work by indexing large number of Web pages. *Web crawlers*, also called "spiders", "robots", or "agents", automatically retrieve Web pages and follow every link they encounter. The content of each Web page is then analyzed to determine how it should be indexed, e.g., words are extracted from the titles, headings, or meta-tags.

When a user enters a query into a search engine, typically by using keywords, it browses its index and provides a list of best-matching Web pages. Most search engines support the use of Boolean operators *and*, *or*, and *not* to further specify the search query.

Search engines have methods to rank the results and to yield the best results first. How a search engine decides which pages are best matches and in what order the results are listed varies widely from one system to another.

While the WWW grows at an increasing pace, its users and content change as well. The Web is no longer only about computer science, routers, and servers. The Web is about people, information, and entertainment; it turns into a *social Web*. This new Web, with its blogs, wikis, and social networks, opens up entirely new opportunities for novel applications and entrepreneurs, and simultaneously introduces new challenges to Web designers and search engines.

Classical keyword-based search engines rely on the fact that the user enters a part of the answer. For example, if you want to know what the tasks of a network protocol are and if you simply enter keywords like "protocol" and "task", then a search engine might yield documents about protocols and tasks, but not necessarily only documents which explain the tasks of protocols. If you knew a part of the answer, e.g., that error-handling is a task of a protocol, you could add the keyword "error-handling" to the query in order to narrow down the search.

1.2.2 Searching Multimedia Knowledge Bases

Multimedia information retrieval (MIR) constitutes a very active multidisciplinary research area that is being transformed into a cross-cutting field. Digital libraries, bio-computing & medical science, the Internet, streaming video, databases, cultural heritage collections, and peer-2-peer networks have created a worldwide need for new paradigms and techniques on how to structure and search multimedia collections. For this reason, MIR systems are one of the most promising fields in the area of information management.

Traditional IR systems only deal with textual and unstructured data. As a result, they are unable to support different kinds of media that are considered typical of a MIR system. For example, multimedia documents are more difficult to index than textual documents, and while metadata is crucial for MIR systems, traditional IR systems do not have such requirement.

The most important feature of a MIR system is the variety of data it must be able to support. Multimedia systems must have the capability to store, retrieve, transport, and present data with very heterogeneous characteristics such as text, images (both still and moving), graphs, and sound. For this reason, the development of a multimedia system is considerably more complex than a traditional information system. Indeed, the latter only deals with simple data types, such as strings or integers, whereas a multimedia system must be able to support objects of very complex structure.

1.2.3 Exploratory Search

Modern IR systems are faced with new challenges. Firstly, there is the increasing complexity of the content, as described above. Secondly, the users' expectations get more exigent and ambitious. For example, it is no longer sufficient that a search engine finds a video document; users expect to get the exact position inside that video. Thirdly, the search behavior of people changes. Generally, users do not know exactly what they are looking for. The search habits of people are still surprisingly old-fashioned, reminiscent of the old days when customers of a library would walk along the shelves and browse through heaps of books.

Today, users still act in a similar way when it comes to computer-assisted searches. The expression *exploratory search* describes users who enter some keywords, randomly click on a link in the result list, inspect that document, which might be a Web page or any other type of document, and quickly decide whether this document is "good" or not. If it is not pertinent, users very frequently enter new keywords without checking other links from the result list [FDD+99, Blo01, HS00].

This paradigm shift of user search behavior requires new knowledge representation and retrieval technologies as well as new retrieval strategies. Some promising technologies have emerged from the Semantic Web movement, e.g., ontologies, Linked Data, Resource Description Framework (RDF), and Web

Ontology Language (OWL). Such technologies allow to describe multimedia documents with machine-readable metadata in a way that applications such as search engines are able to process and integrate into their processes.

For a search engine, the meaning of content is more important than the content itself. Also, the interpretation and the disambiguation of data get more reliable when a machine is able to "understand" the meaning of a query. Structured vocabularies and external language sources, such as dictionaries or thesauri, are used for processing natural language (NL) query terms.

Modern *expert systems* have optimized search functionalities over online and offline domain knowledge bases, turning them into reliable and helpful companions. An E-Librarian Service, which we discuss in great detail in this book, is an example of such a system.

1.3 E-Librarian Services

1.3.1 Overview

An E-Librarian Service is a computer system that is able to retrieve multimedia resources from a knowledge base more efficiently than if it were to browse through an index or perform a simple keyword search. The premise is that more pertinent results would be retrieved if the *semantic search engine* "understood" the sense of the user query and was able to reason over the data. The returned results would then be logical consequences of an inference rather than of keyword matching.

An E-Librarian Service allows users to enter complete questions in NL and retrieves only few, but semantically pertinent answers. It is able to generalize or specialize the query in order to find the most appropriate document(s) in its multimedia knowledge base. This is particularly interesting if the system finds out that there is no document that will deliver a complete answer. In this case, the E-Librarian Service identifies and retrieves documents that are semantically closest to the query, based on the premise that people always expect an answer, even if it is not a perfect one.

An E-Librarian Service does not return the answer to the user question, but it retrieves the most pertinent document(s) in which the user can find the answer to his question. For example, let us suppose that the user asked the following question:

$$\text{What are the tasks of a protocol?} \tag{1.1}$$

Just like a human librarian, the E-Librarian Service would then deliver a document in which the user finds the answer to his question. This librarian approach to solving complex retrieval problems will be described in more detail in section 1.3.4.

An E-Librarian Service is an ontology-driven expert system about a given domain, e.g., computer history, fractions in mathematics, or networks in computer science. It relies on specialized and hierarchically organized knowledge bases and specific reasoning services. The documents in the knowledge base are described by metadata that is encoded in a knowledge representation formalism, like the *Web Ontology Language* (OWL).

1.3.2 Early Question-Answering Systems

Question-answering (QA) is a type of IR. Given a collection of documents, such as the WWW or a local database, the system should be able to retrieve answers to questions asked in NL. QA is regarded as requiring more complex natural language processing (NLP) techniques than other types of IR, such as document retrieval, and it is sometimes considered the next step beyond search engines.

Some of the early artificial intelligence systems developed in the 1960s, such as *Baseball* and *Lunar*, were QA systems. *Baseball* answered questions about the US baseball league over a period of one year. *Lunar* answered questions about the geological analysis of rocks returned by the Apollo moon missions. It was demonstrated at a lunar science convention in 1971 and it was able to answer 90% of the questions in its domain asked by people unfamiliar with the system.

The 1970s and 1980s saw the development of comprehensive theories in computational linguistics which led to the development of ambitious projects in text comprehension and QA. One example of such a system was the *Unix Consultant* [WAC84], a system that answered questions pertaining to the Unix operating system. The system had a comprehensive hand-crafted knowledge base of its domain and it aimed at phrasing the answer to accommodate various types of users. The system developed in the Unix Consultant project never went past the stage of simple demonstrations, but it helped the development of theories on computational linguistics and reasoning.

1.3.3 Natural Language Interface

The interaction between humans and computers is still surprisingly complicated. Finding information in a knowledge base often means browsing through an index or formulating computer-readable queries. In both cases, the users must adapt themselves to the machine by entering precise and machine-readable instructions.

However, most people are not search experts and therefore have difficulties when it comes to formulating their queries in a machine-optimized way, e.g., by combining search terms with Boolean operators. Furthermore, they might not use the right domain expressions, which but adds to the complexity of the problem.

An NL interface simplifies the human-machine interaction. An E-Librarian Service allows users to freely formulate questions in NL, which allows them to focus on *what* they want, rather than to worry about *how* and *where* to obtain the answer.

In order to create an "intelligent" search mechanism, the user must enter a query which contains enough semantics, so that the E-Librarian Service "understands" the sense of the question and is able to logically infer over the knowledge base. A complete question in NL contains more semantics than just keywords. An E-Librarian Service uses linguistic information within the user question and the given context from the domain ontology in order to "understand" the sense of the sentence and to translate it into a logical form.

1.3.4 No Library without a Librarian

Let us suppose that Paul wants to find out some information about the invention of the transistor. He goes to a library and asks the librarian: "I want to know who invented the transistor." The librarian perfectly understands Paul's question and knows where to find the right book. He also understands that Paul does not want all the available books in the library that explain how a transistor works, or those which illustrate in detail the lives of its inventor(s). It is evident for the librarian that Paul only wants one pertinent document in which he can find the answer to his question. This illustration leads to the following statements:

For the client:

- Paul formulates his question in NL.
- Paul has no knowledge about the internal organization of the books in the library.
- Paul does not know what he is looking for in particular, e.g., he does not give the librarian a precise book title.

For the librarian:

- He is able to understand the client's question (both language and meaning).
- He does not know the answer to the client's question.
- He controls the internal organization of the library.
- From all the existing books in the library, he finds the one(s) that best fit(s) the needs of the client.

It is obvious that the larger the library is, the more documents will be potentially pertinent, especially if general questions are asked. If Paul wants to be sure that he will only get a very short list of relevant books, then he should formulate a more precise question or go to a specialized library. There, the potential amount of documents is far smaller, but the chance of finding pertinent results is higher. Visiting specialized libraries also reduces the risk of ambiguity. If Paul asked for a book about "dragons" in a general library, the librarian would have the choice between a mythical creature and a musket. However, if Paul were in a library dedicated to weaponry, the context would be clear.

1.3.5 Characteristics of an E-Librarian Service

An E-Librarian Service is a computer-based expert system that offers the same services as a real librarian. The core part of an E-Librarian Service is an MIR module that performs a semantic search over the knowledge base. It retrieves only few but semantically pertinent documents as an answer to the users' questions. One should not confuse it with a software to manage a library or with a search engine over a catalogue.

Unlike classical search engines or QA systems, an E-Librarian Service does not deliver the answer to the user's question, but it is able to find and retrieve the most pertinent document(s), in which the user will then find the answer to his question.

Let us stretch out the difference between both approaches. The first category of retrieval systems seeks to provide concise and succinct answers to NL questions. The aim of such search engines or QA systems is to perform fine-grained, targeted IR. For example, let us consider the following question:

$$\textit{Who invented the transistor?} \qquad (1.2)$$

A QA system should return a precise answer, i.e., the names of the inventors of the transistor: William Shockley, John Bardeen, and Walter Houser Brattain.

The second category of retrieval systems, to which E-Librarian Services belong, implement strategies for extracting documents or sub-parts of documents that contain the answer to the query. Such retrieval strategies are generally known as *passage retrieval*. They have been used in classical IR systems over textual documents and have proven effective when documents are of a considerable length or when there are topic changes within a document.

An E-Librarian Service is a reliable and easy-to-use expert system that allows users to find pertinent resources in a multimedia repository very quickly. Its concept adheres to the stream of the Semantic Web philosophy and joins the efforts to standardize and link reusable multimedia content, ontologies, and technologies.

An E-Librarian Service improves domain ontology search engines; fewer, yet more pertinent results are returned, as will be demonstrated when we present different applications as "best practices".

An E-Librarian Service can easily be used in other areas, such as online helpdesks or travel planners. Clients requiring assistance, e.g., with their Internet connection, or with itineraries, could contact a "virtual online help desk" and express questions in NL. The E-Librarian Service will then "understand" the gist of the customers' questions and suggest short, but pertinent answers.

Here is a summary of the characteristics of an E-Librarian Service:

- It has a huge amount of stored knowledge in multimedia form.
- It controls the internal organization of its knowledge base.
- It "understands" the gist of the user questions.
- A query is expressed in NL.
- Given a query, it finds pertinent documents in its knowledge base.
- It is able to visualize the pertinence of the delivered documents, i.e., ranking of the results according to their semantic relatedness to the query.
- It is simply accessible without complicated software or hardware requirements.
- It is simple to use, i.e., the interaction takes place in a human way by means of verbal communication.

1.4 Overview and Organization of the Book

This book focuses on the design, implementation, and testing of a novel approach to retrieval systems by regrouping the most appropriate theories and technologies from different research domains. It also described the required technologies, strategies and technical details on how to develop an E-Librarian Service.

This book is structured as follows:

- Part 1 presents the technologies required to build an E-Librarian Service. In chapter 2, the Semantic Web and its underlying technologies (ontologies, XML, RDF, and OWL) are explained. Chapter 3 focuses on Description Logics as formal knowledge representation language. An introduction to NLP and to IR is given in chapters 4 and 5..
- Part 2 of this book is dedicated to the design and implementation of an E-Librarian Service. Chapter 6 focuses on the ontological approach and the creation of metadata, while chapter 7 describes how to develop the NLP module. The design of the MIR module, i.e., the semantic search engine is explained in chapter 8. Implementation details are described in chapter 9.
- Part 3 of this book illustrates three best practices of E-Librarian Services that were tested in real life scenarios. These are the *Computer History expert system* (CHESt), *Mathematics expert system* (MatES), and the Lecture Butler's E-Librarian Service.
- Part 4 concludes this book with an appendix of different resources that are not mentioned in the main content.

Part I

Key Technologies of E-Librarian Services

2

Semantic Web and Ontologies

The Semantic Web is an evolving extension of the World Wide Web in which Web content can be expressed not only in natural language, but also in a form that can be read and "understood" by software agents, thus permitting them to find, share, and integrate information more easily. It derives from Tim Berners-Lee's vision of the Web as a universal medium for data, information, and knowledge exchange.

At its core, the Semantic Web comprises a philosophy, a set of design principles, collaborative working groups, and a variety of enabling technologies. Some elements of the Semantic Web are expressed as prospective future possibilities that have yet to be implemented or realized. Other elements are expressed in formal specifications, like the *Resource Description Framework* (RDF) and the *Web Ontology Language* (OWL).

2.1 What is the Semantic Web?

The aim of this section is to focus on the scientific dimension of the Semantic Web and its extensions as seen by the World Wide Web Consortium (W3C)[1]. The evolutionary path of the "classical" World Wide Web (WWW) towards a better Web is given in [MS04]. A more complete view of the Semantic Web architecture and related technologies can be found in: [BCT07, PB06, HKR10, AvH04, AH08, MS11a, MS11b].

2.1.1 The Vision of the Semantic Web

The WWW is a place where there is a huge amount of information. In that Web, machines are charged with the presentation of the information, which is a relatively simple task and people have to do the linking and interpreting, e.g., when trying to find the information they are looking for, which is a

---

[1] http://www.w3.org/2001/sw/

much harder task. The obvious question is: "Why not get computers to do more of the hard work?" That statement is representative for the discussion toward a new Web that was popularized by Tim Berners-Lee under the name of *Semantic Web* [BLHL01].

> The Semantic Web will bring structure to the meaningful content of Web pages, creating an environment where software agents roaming from page to page can readily carry out sophisticated tasks for users. [...]
> The Semantic Web is not a separate Web but an extension of the current one, in which information is given well-defined meaning, better enabling computers and people to work in cooperation. [...]
> In the near future, these developments will usher in significant new functionality as machines become much better able to process and "understand" the data that they merely display at present.

The Semantic Web is about two things. Firstly, it is about common formats for integration and combination of data drawn from heterogeneous sources, whereas on the original Web mainly concentrated on the interchange of documents. Thus, the Semantic Web is often presented as being one huge database or a set of distributed databases. Secondly, it is also about language for recording how the data relates to real world objects. This allows a person or a machine to start off in one database and then move through an unending set of databases, which are connected not by wires, but by the fact that they are about the same thing.

2.1.2 Semantic Web vs. Web *n*.0

There are a lot of different expressions and buzzwords for the alternative evolving extension of the WWW, e.g., *Web of the Next Generation*, *Social Web*, and more popular expressions like *Web 2.0* and *Web 3.0*. There is considerable debate about what the Web *n*.0 terms actually mean.

The phrase *Web 2.0* was coined in 2003 by O'Reilly Media[2]. It hints at an improved form of the WWW based on technologies such as Web blogs, social bookmarking, wikis, podcasts, RSS feeds, social software, Web APIs, Web standards, social networks, and online Web services. Sometimes, *Web 2.0* is also used as synonym for *Social Web*.

The term *Web 3.0* first appeared prominently in early 2006 in a blog article by Jeffrey Zeldman[3]. It has been coined with different meanings to describe the evolution of Web usage and interaction along several separate

---

[2] http://radar.oreilly.com/archives/2006/05/controversy_about_our_web_20_s.html

[3] http://www.alistapart.com/articles/web3point0

paths. These include transforming the WWW into a database, a move towards making content accessible by multiple non-browser applications, the leveraging of artificial intelligence technologies and the Semantic Web, and three dimensional interaction and collaboration. Generally, *Web 3.0* is seen as "Semantic, Social, Service Web", and *Web of the next decade.*

2.1.3 Three Principles Ruling the Semantic Web

At its very base, the Semantic Web relies on the following principles:

- The Semantic Web is about *resources* (and not limited to Web pages like in the classical WWW). A resource can literally be anything, e.g., a Web page, a book, or a human being.
- Every resource is identified by a *Uniform Resource Identifier* (URI). URIs are short ASCII-strings that identify resources. Hence, a URI can be the address of a Web page (URL), the ISBN of a book, or the social security number of a person. *Internationalized Resource Identifiers* (IRIs) are a complement to URIs. An IRI is a sequence of characters from the *Universal Character Set* (Unicode), e.g., to use Chinese symbols in a URI.
- Resources on the Semantic Web are described with additional information, called *metadata*. Metadata are expressed in a formal language like XML, RDF, or OWL.

2.1.4 Architecture

The classical WWW appeared without an initial plan or *roadmap*. It has been growing since its beginning in an uncontrolled way. New technologies issued from research projects and some became de facto standards or were standardized later. Such extensions and technologies were not interpreted or implemented in all browsers in the same way.

Due to this lack of design in the early years of the WWW, a roadmap was elaborated to build the Semantic Web bottom up. That roadmap suggests a layered architecture, where each layer improves the underlaying layer with new features and technologies.

As the Semantic Web is still ongoing research, the roadmap was updated in the past years. Figure 2.1 depicts its architecture, the so called *Layer Cake*. The lower layers URI, XML, RDF, OWL, and SPARQL have achieved the state of W3C recommendations. The *Semantic Web Rule Language* (SWRL) is submitted to the W3C and is currently being finalized. The upper layers Logic, Proof, and Trust are still ongoing research. The Logic layer enables the writing of rules, while the Proof layer executes the rules and evaluates together with the Trust layer mechanism for applications whether to trust the given proof or not. These upper layers present some of the most difficult technical challenges faced by the Semantic Web venture.

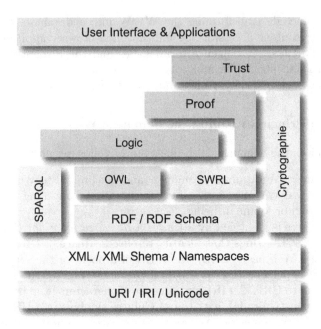

Fig. 2.1. Semantic Web architecture, the so called *Layer Cake*.

2.2 Ontologies

Ontologies are seen as a key component of the Semantic Web. They are used as a form of knowledge representation about the world or some part of it. The term *ontology* has its origin in philosophy, where it is the name of one fundamental branch of metaphysics concerned with analyzing various types or modes of existence.

In both computer science and information science, an ontology is a data model that represents a set of concepts within a domain and the relationships between those concepts. It is used to reason about the objects within that domain.

ontologies are built with a specific language, e.g., XML, RDF, or OWL. Depending on the level of expressivity needed by a developer, the best suitable language can be chosen.

2.2.1 Ontology Structure

In computer science, "an ontology is an explicit, formal specification of a shared conceptualization" [Gru93]. Also, "ontologies are formal and consensual specifications of conceptualizations that provide a shared understanding of a domain, an understanding that can be communicated across people and application systems" [Fen04]. What ontology has in common in both computer science and philosophy is the representation of entities (individuals) and ideas (classes), along with their properties (attributes) and relations.

Individuals

Individuals (instances) are the basic, "ground level" components of an ontology. The individuals in an ontology may include concrete objects such as people, animals, tables, automobiles, molecules, and planets, as well as abstract individuals such as numbers and words.

Classes

Classes (concepts) are abstract groups, sets, or collections of objects. They may contain individuals, other classes, or a combination of both. Importantly, a class can subsume or be subsumed by other classes. With respect to the hierarchy of classes depicted in figure 3.1, Person subsumes Actor, since anything that is a member of the latter class is a member of the former.

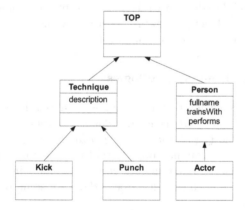

Fig. 2.2. Class hierarchy (taxonomy) using the UML formalism.

Attributes

Individuals and classes in an ontology can be described by assigning attributes (properties) to them. Attributes over classes have a name and attributes over individuals have in addition a value that is used to store information that is specific to the individual.

For instance, the class Actor has the (inherited) attributes fullname, trainsWith and performs. Therefore, the individual Actor(SergeLinckels) has, among other things, the attribute fullname with the value "Serge Linckels". The value of an attribute can be a literal or a complex datatype. A complex datatype can be, e.g., a list of values and not just a single value.

Relationships

An important use of attributes is to describe the relationships between objects in the ontology. There are two types of relations. The first and most important type is the *subsumption relation*, commonly called "is-a". This defines which objects are members of classes. For example, Human subsumes Woman, therefore Woman is a Human.

The addition of the is-a relationships has created a hierarchical taxonomy; a tree-like structure that clearly depicts how objects relate to one another (see figure 3.1). In such a structure, each class is the *child class* (subclass) of a *parent class* (superclass), typically with the most general class at the top and very specific classes at the bottom. Most often TOP is a built-in class (`rdfs:Resource` in RDF and `owl:Thing` in OWL).

The second type of relation is user defined relations, e.g., the relation performs from the class Person to the class Technique or the reflexive relation trainsWith from the class Person to itself. In the first example, the emerging structure is a directed acyclic graph, whereas in the second example, the emerging structure is a directed cyclic graph.

2.2.2 Upper- and Domain Ontologies

According to their range and domain of application, ontologies can be divided into two categories: *upper ontologies* and *domain ontologies*.

An **Upper Ontology** (*World Ontology, Top Ontology* or *Foundation Ontology*) is a model of the common objects that are generally applicable across a wide range of domains. It contains a core vocabulary in whose terms objects in a set of domains can be described. Here are some popular examples of Upper Ontologies:

- The *Dublin Core*[4] (DC) metadata element set is a standard for cross-domain information resource description. It provides a simple and standardized set of conventions for describing things in ways that make them easier to find. Dublin Core is widely used to describe digital materials such as video, sound, image, text, and composite media like Web pages.
- *OpenCyc*[5] includes hundreds of thousands of terms along with millions of assertions relating the terms to each other. One stated goal is that of providing a completely free and unrestricted semantic vocabulary for use in the Semantic Web. The OpenCyc taxonomy is available in OWL.

---

[4] http://dublincore.org/
[5] http://www.opencyc.org/

- *Suggested Upper Merged Ontology* (SUMO)[6] was developed within the IEEE Standard Upper Ontology Working Group. The goal is to develop a standard ontology that will promote data interoperability, information search and retrieval, automated inferencing, and natural language processing.
- *Gene Ontology* (GO)[7] is a major bioinformatics initiative with the aim of standardizing the representation of gene and gene product attributes across species and databases. The project provides a controlled vocabulary of terms for describing gene product characteristics and gene product annotation data, as well as tools to access and process this data.

A **domain ontology** models a specific domain or part of the world. It represents the particular meanings of terms as they apply to that domain. For example, the word "date" has many different meanings. An ontology about the domain of fruits would model the "sweet, dark brown, oval fruit containing a hard stone, often eaten dried" meaning of the word, while an ontology about the domain of American history would model the "day on a calendar" meaning. Here are some examples of domain ontologies:

- The famous *Wine Ontology*[8] is about the most appropriate combination of wine and meals.
- The *Soccer Ontology*[9] describes most concepts that are specific to soccer: players, rules, field, supporters, actions, etc. It is used to annotate videos in order to produce personalized summary of soccer matches.
- The *National Cancer Institute thesaurus*[10] is a public domain description logic-based terminology [HdCD⁺05]. The semantic relationships in the thesaurus are intended to facilitate translational research and to support the bioinformatics infrastructure. Topics described in the ontology include diseases, drugs, chemicals, diagnoses, genes, treatments, anatomy, organisms, and proteins.
- The *Music Ontology*[11] provides main concepts and properties for describing music (e.g., artists, albums, tracks, performances, and arrangements).

2.2.3 Linked Data

Domain ontologies represent concepts in very specific and often eclectic ways. Current research in *ontology engineering* aims to create specialized ontologies for every imaginable domain. This allows developers to reuse existing ontologies and to concentrate on their application rather than on the datastructure;

---

[6] http://www.ontologyportal.org/
[7] http://www.geneontology.org/
[8] http://www.w3.org/TR/owl-guide/wine.rdf
[9] http://www.daml.org/ontologies/273
[10] ftp://ftp1.nci.nih.gov/pub/cacore/EVS/
[11] http://musicontology.com/

they simply use something that was proven correct and extensible. Ontology engineering, in analogy to software engineering, is concerned with the challenges of designing ontologies by providing methodologies and tools for their development, evaluation, and maintenance [GPCGFL03, SS04, HKR10, BCT07, Haf10, ES07, Stu09].

As systems that rely on domain ontologies expand, they often need to merge domain ontologies into a more general representation. This presents a challenge to the ontology engineer. Different ontologies in the same domain can also arise due to different perceptions of the domain based on cultural background, education, ideology, or because a different representation language was chosen.

Today, there exists a large number and a wide range of different ontologies. An emerging challenge is the linking of ontologies. For illustration, consider that in library A, *Dublin Core* is used to describe the content of the repository and a different vocabulary is used in library B. Hence, the exchange of information on a semantic level between both libraries would not be possible easily.

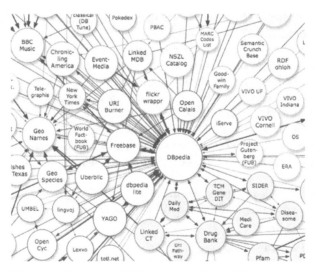

Fig. 2.3. Datasets published in the Linked Data format.

The need to link semantic databases initiated the *Linked Data* movement which aims to connect related data that was not previously linked. The *Linked Open Data* project by the W3C is to extend the Web with a data commons by publishing various open datasets in a standardized format, i.e., RDF. Furthermore, links between these different data sources are set. In the Link Open Data project, the *DBPedia* plays a central role as it makes the content of Wikipedia available in RDF (see figure 2.3). The importance of DBPedia is not only that it includes Wikipedia data, but also that it incorporates links to other datasets on the Web. By providing those extra links, applications may exploit the extra (and possibly more precise) knowledge from other datasets when developing an application.

2.2.4 Expressivity of Ontologies

Information can be expressed in a more or less complex way, depending on the level of expressivity needed. As ontologies are used to model information of the real world, they can be categorized according to their level of expressivity (see figure 2.4) [LM01].

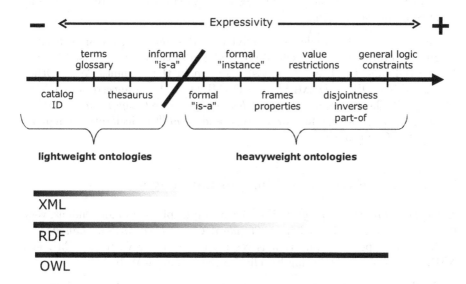

Fig. 2.4. Expressivity of ontologies.

Lightweight Ontologies

- A controlled vocabulary is a finite list of terms. Catalogs are an example of this category because they can provide an unambiguous interpretation of terms.
- A glossary is a list of terms and meanings expressed in natural language.
- thesauri provide some additional semantics in their relations between terms, e.g., synonym relationships.
- Ontologies of the category "informal is-a" provide a notion of generalization and specialization with a small number of top-level classes. Such ontologies do not provide strict subclass or "is-a" relationships.

Heavyweight Ontologies

- ontologies "formal is-a" provide taxonomies with formal "is-a" relationships.
- Ontologies "formal instance" include formal instance relationships and instance checking.
- While considering frames, properties of classes can include properties that can be inherited.
- Ontologies "value restriction" provide value restrictions to specify what can fill a property.
- More complex expressions over classes and properties require operations like disjointness, inverse and part-of.
- Very expressive ontology languages allow to specify first order logic constraints between terms.

According to the needed expressivity of the ontology, an appropriated language to formalize its specifications and conceptualizations must be used. XML, RDF and OWL are the most common in the Semantic Web. Other languages like OIL[12], DAML[13], and DAML+OIL[14] are ancestors of OWL. More specific languages are, e.g., the *Knowledge Interchange Format* (KIF)[15] to serve as a syntax for first-order logic and *CycL*[16] a declarative language used in the Cyc project.

2.3 XML – Extensible Markup Language

Extensible Markup Language[17] (XML) is a simple, platform independent, very flexible text format derived from *Standard Generalized Markup Language*[18] (SGML). No special application is required to read or write an XML file. XML introduces the following benefits to the Semantic Web:

- XML allows to describe a resource with metadata in a structured way.
- The metadata created with XML is pure text, therefore it is machine-readable.
- Additionally, *XML Schema*[19] provides a means for defining the structure, content and syntax of XML documents.

This section gives an overview of XML. More exhaustive explanations can be found, e.g., in [MS04, HM02, AvH04].

---

[12] http://www.ontoknowledge.org/oil/
[13] http://www.daml.org/
[14] http://www.daml.org/2001/03/daml+oil-index
[15] http://suo.ieee.org/SUO/KIF/suo-kif.html
[16] http://www.cyc.com/cycdoc/ref/cycl-syntax.html
[17] http://www.w3.org/XML/
[18] http://www.w3.org/MarkUp/SGML/
[19] http://www.w3.org/XML/Schema

2.3.1 XML: Elements, Attributes and Values

An XML document is built with *elements*, also called *tags*. In the example below, elements are `actor`, `fullname`, and `trainsWith`. The elements `fullname` and `trainsWith` are nested in the element `actor`; we say that `fullname` and `trainsWith` are child-elements of `actor`.

```
<actor idActor="http://www.linckels.lu/">
  <fullname>Serge Linckels</fullname>
  <performs>yop chagi</performs>
</actor>
```

Element names can include letters (a..z, A..Z), digits (0..9), the punctuation chars underscore (_), hyphen (-) and period (.), as well as special characters like ö, ç, and Ω. Element names are case sensitive, e.g., `actor` $\neq$ `Actor`.

An element can be used several times, e.g., there could be multiple elements `actor`. Each element can have a value, e.g., the value of the element `fullname` is "Serge Linckels".

Elements can also have *attributes*. In the above example, the element `actor` has the attribute `idActor`. Each attribute must have a value that is always given within quotes (simple or double). In the example, the attribute `idActor` has the value "http://www.linckels.lu/".

The decision whether some information is represented using elements or attributes is semantically irrelevant. Therefore, the following XML-code is semantically equivalent to the one above:

```
<actor fullname="Serge Linckels" performs="yop chagi">
  <idActor>http://www.linckels.lu/</idActor>
</actor>
```

All elements must be correctly nested; we say that the XML document is *well-formed*. This requires that all elements be closed in the right order, e.g., `<a><b></a></b>` is not well-formed, whereas `<a><b></b></a>` is well-formed. Every element must be closed, even if there is no explicit end-element, e.g,

```
<idActor location="http://www.linckels.lu/" />.
```

A parser can be used to check if an XML document is well-formed. A simple way of parsing a XML document is to open it in a Web browser; if it is displayed correctly, then the XML document is well-formed.

An XML file is pure text, but can use different encodings, e.g, ASCII, Latin-1, Unicode, UTF-8, or ISO-8859-1. When this parameter is omitted, then Unicode is used by default. Unicode has 95156 characters from most living languages on earth. The used encoding is specified in the first line of the XML file:

```
<?xml version="1.0" encoding="UTF-8" ?>.
```

2.3.2 Namespaces and Qualified Names

Sometimes, element names can be confusing. Consider the following example:

```
<picture>
  <name>Taekwondo picture</name>
  <actor name="http://www.linckels.lu/">
    <name>Serge Linckels</name>
  </actor>
</picture>
```

Here, `name` is used in both elements `picture` and `actor`. Additionally, `name` is also used as an attribute in the element `actor`. To solve this ambiguity, element names can be prefixed in order to use *qualified names*.

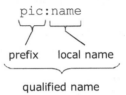

A prefix is defined in a *namespace*. The used namespaces must be indicated in the top-element of the document using the attribute `xmlns`. Each namespace has a URI, which is a purely formal identifier. This means that no physical file must exist at that URI. Namespaces only apply to elements, not to attributes. The above example could be written as follows whilst using qualified names:

```
<demo:picture
  xmlns:demo="http://www.linckels.lu/demo/demo"
  xmlns:act="http://www.linckels.lu/demo/actor">
  <pic:name>Taekwondo picture</pic:name>
  <act:actor name="http://www.linckels.lu/">
    <act:name>Serge Linckels</act:name>
  </act:actor>
</demo:picture>
```

2.3.3 XML Schema

XML Schema is an XML document containing a formal description of what comprises a valid XML document. XML Schema allows to express rules, which element- and attribute names can be used, which datatypes the values must have (see appendix A), which element can be nested into what other element, etc. An XML document described by a schema is called an *instance document*. A validating parser[20] can then be used to check if a XML document is *valid* according a given XML Schema.

---

[20] For example: `http://www.w3schools.com/xml/xml_validator.asp`

```
<xs:schema xmlns:xs="http://www.w3.org/2001/XMLSchema">
  <xs:complexType name="actor">
    <xs:sequence>
      <xs:element name="fullname" type="xs:string"
        use="required" />
      <xs:element name="performs" type="xs:string"
             minOccurs="0" maxOccurs="unbound" />
    </xs:sequence>
    <xs:attribute name="idActor"
                   type="xs:anyURI" use="required"/>
  </xs:complexType>
</xs:schema>
```

The above XML Schema defines a parent-element actor, with the attribute idActor. That attribute is required (use="required") and has a URI as value (type="xs:anyURI). Furthermore, the element actor has two child-elements: fullname and performs both of the datatype string.

The child-element fullname is mandatory (as indicated by the attribute use; if the parameter use is omitted, then the default value is optional) and the element can appear zero or one time inside the parent-element. To specify that an element can be repeated several times, the attributes minOccurs and maxOccurs must be used. The default values of both attributes is 1. In the example, an actor can perform zero or more techniques.

A complex element is an element that nests child-elements, like actor. It is defined using the element complexType followed by a specification about how the complex content is to be parsed. There are three possibilities:

- **sequence**: the list of elements must appear in the target document in the exact order they are given,
- **all**: the order does not matter in which the list of elements appear in the target document,
- **choice**: only one element from the list can appear in the target document.

Instead of XML Schema, Document Type Definition (DTD) can be used to describe the structure of an XML document. XML Schema have more powerful capabilities, but DTD are still used in many applications.

2.3.4 Complete Example

Suppose that figure 2.5 has the URI http://www.linckels.lu/kick.jpg. Although this is a Web address (URL), the picture must not necessarily be physically at that location; the URI is simply a formal identifier of a resource and not its actual location.

The picture could be described as follows: *This picture shows two sports-men performing kicks. Serge Linckels performs a kick called "yop chagi" and David Arendt performs a kick called "dollyo chagi"*. Translated into XML, this description could be as follows:

Fig. 2.5. What is the meaning of this picture?

```xml
<?xml version="1.0" encoding="UTF-8" ?>
<picture idPicture="http://www.linckels.lu/kick.jpg">
  <title>Two sportsmen performing kicks</title>
  <actors>
    <actor idActor="http://www.linckels.lu/">
      <fullname>Serge Linckels</fullname>
      <performs idKick="kick1" />
    </actor>
    <actor idActor="19780329123">
      <fullname>David Arendt</fullname>
      <performs idKick="kick2" />
    </actor>
  </actors>
  <techniques>
    <kick idKick="kick1">
      <description>yop chagi</description>
    </kick>
    <kick idKick="kick2">
      <description>dollyo chagi</description>
    </kick>
  </techniques>
</picture>
```

The according XML Schema would the be as follows:

```xml
<?xml version="1.0"?>
<xs:schema xmlns:xs="http://www.w3.org/2001/XMLSchema">
  <xs:element name="picture" type="picture_type" />
  <xs:complexType name="picture_type">
    <xs:sequence>
      <xs:element name="title" type="xs:string"/>
      <xs:element name="actors" type="actors_type"/>
      <xs:element name="techniques" type="techniques_type"/>
    </xs:sequence>
    <xs:attribute name="idPicture"
                  type="xs:anyURI" use="required"/>
  </xs:complexType>
  <xs:complexType name="actors_type">
    <xs:sequence>
      <xs:element name="actor" type="actor_type"
                  minOccurs="0" maxOccurs="unbounded" />
    </xs:sequence>
  </xs:complexType>
  <xs:complexType name="actor_type">
    <xs:sequence>
      <xs:element name="fullname" type="xs:string" />
      <xs:element name="performs">
        <xs:complexType>
          <xs:attribute name="idKick" type="xs:anyURI"
                        use="optional"/>
        </xs:complexType>
      </xs:element>
    </xs:sequence>
    <xs:attribute name="idActor" type="xs:anyURI"
                  use="required"/>
  </xs:complexType>
  <xs:complexType name="techniques_type">
    <xs:sequence>
      <xs:element name="kick" type="kick_type"
                  minOccurs="0" maxOccurs="unbounded" />
    </xs:sequence>
  </xs:complexType>
  <xs:complexType name="kick_type">
    <xs:sequence>
      <xs:element name="description" type="xs:string" />
    </xs:sequence>
    <xs:attribute name="idKick" type="xs:anyURI"
                  use="required"/>
  </xs:complexType>
</xs:schema>
```

2.3.5 Limitations of XML

XML describes some meaning of a resource in a structured way, e.g., it provides structured metadata about a picture. However, XML lacks expressiveness when it comes to complex relations and restrictions of relations, e.g., in the above example, we cannot easily express what the relation between an actor and a kick is, or how many kicks an actor can perform.

2.4 RDF – Resource Description Framework

Resource Description Framework[21] (RDF) has been a W3C recommendation since 2004. It is based upon the idea of making statements about resources in the form of *subject-predicate-object* expressions, called *triples*. The subject denotes the resource. The predicate denotes a property of the resource and expresses a relationship between the subject and the object.

This mechanism for describing resources is a major component of the Semantic Web activity and has the following benefits:

- RDF allows to describe relations between resources in a more expressive way than XML.
- RDF can be serialized as XML (or in other formats like *Notation 3*[22] or *N-Triples*[23]).
- *RDF Schema*[24] provides a means for defining the structure, content and syntax of RDF documents.
- RDF documents can be queried using optimized query languages, e.g., SPARQL[25] (see section 2.5.4).

This section gives an overview of RDF. More exhaustive explanations can be found, e.g., in [AH08, Pow03, Hje01, HKR10, BCT07, AvH04].

2.4.1 RDF Triples and Serialization

RDF allows to describe resources in a more expressive way than XML by formulating statements about resources. Every statement is composed of three parts: a *subject* (resource), a *predicate* (a property of the resource), and an *object* (the value of the property). Therefore, an RDF statement is called a triple.

As an example, a statement could be that the resource identified by the URI http://www.linckels.lu/ has the name "Serge Linckels". Here,

---

[21] http://www.w3.org/RDF/

[22] http://www.w3.org/DesignIssues/Notation3

[23] http://www.w3.org/2001/sw/RDFCore/ntriples/

[24] http://www.w3.org/XML/Schema

[25] http://www.w3.org/TR/rdf-sparql-query/

the subject is the resource (`http://www.linckels.lu/`), the predicate is
`fullname`, and the object is "Serge Linckels". In this case, the object of
this triple is a literal. But predicates can also connect two resources, e.g., to
express that the resource identified by the URI `http://www.linckels.lu/`
trains with the resource identified by the URI 19780329123. Here, the predicate `trainsWith` has as object another resource.

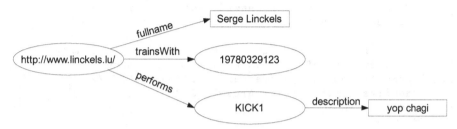

Fig. 2.6. RDF graph representing four triples.

RDF triples can be represented as directed graph. Generally, resources are
represented by ellipses, properties by arrows and literals as rectangles. The
RDF graph depicted in figure 2.6 represents the following four statements:

Subject	Predicate	Object
http://www.linckels.lu/	fullname	"Serge Linckels" (literal)
http://www.linckels.lu/	trainsWith	19780329123 (resource)
http://www.linckels.lu/	performs	KICK1 (resource)
KICK1	description	"yop chagi" (literal)

RDF triples can be serialized as XML documents (or other formalisms like
Turtle or *Manchester Syntax*) to make them machine-readable. Every RDF
element exists in the RDF namespace[26]. Resources are described using the
element `Description` with the attribute `about` to define the resource's URI.
Properties are user-defined child-elements of `Description`.

In our example, we define properties in the namespace `demo`. Of course,
existing vocabularies could be used, like *Dublin Core*[27] (dc) or *Friend of a
Friend*[28] (foaf), as explained in section 2.2.3. If a predicate refers to another
resource (and not to a literal), then the URI of the referenced resource is
specified by the attribute `resource`.

The following code shows the XML serialization of the RDF graph depicted
in figure 2.6.

---

[26] `http://www.w3.org/1999/02/22-rdf-syntax-ns`
[27] `http://dublincore.org/`
[28] `http://www.foaf-project.org/`

```
<rdf:RDF
  xmlns:rdf="http://www.w3.org/1999/02/22-rdf-syntax-ns#"
  xmlns:demo="http://www.linckels.lu/demo/">

  <rdf:Description rdf:about="19780329123" />

  <rdf:Description rdf:about="KICK1">
    <demo:description>yop chagi</demo:description>
  </rdf:Description>

  <rdf:Description rdf:about="http://www.linckels.lu/">
    <demo:fullname>Serge Linckels</demo:fullname>
    <demo:trainsWith rdf:resource="19780329123" />
    <demo:performs rdf:resource="KICK1" />
  </rdf:Description>
</rdf:RDF>
```

A parser can be used to check the validity of an RDF/XML document with respect to the official RDF specification. The online *W3C Validator*[29] checks the syntax of the documents and returns the according triples as RDF graph.

2.4.2 RDF Schema

RDF Schema[30] is an extensible knowledge representation language, providing basic elements for the description of ontologies intended to structure RDF resources. It allows to define classes and properties belonging to these classes using the elements class and Property. In the example depicted in figure 2.7, rdfs:Resource, Technique and Person are classes, and description, fullname, trainsWith and performs are properties.

The qualified name of a class is defined by the attribute about. The element subClassOf is used to define sub-class relationships. Its attribute rdf:resource specifies the URI of the super-class. The standard top-class is rdfs:Resource in the RDF syntax. Inheritance only applies to classes, not to properties.

The qualified name of a property is defined by the attribute about. Properties are not nested inside classes. Therefore, the element domain is required to specify the class to which the property belongs. Optionally, the element range defines the class which the property references. This can be another user-defined class, like in our example, to specify that a "Person" performs a "Technique". The range-element can also be used to specify a standard XML datatype, e.g., integer or string.

---

[29] http://www.w3.org/RDF/Validator/
[30] http://www.w3.org/TR/rdf-schema/

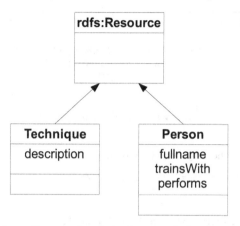

Fig. 2.7. UML formalism to show inheritance relation between RDF classes.

An instance of a class is nothing else than a resource. Hence, to create an instance of a class, e.g., the Person "Serge Linckels", the name of the class must be indicated as shown below.

The following two examples are equal; in example 1, the type is explicitly specified by the element **type**, whereas example 2 depicts a shortened version by replacing the element **Description** with the class-name.

```
<rdf:Description rdf:about="http://www.linckels.lu/">
   <demo:fullname>Serge Linckels</demo:fullname>
   <rdf:type
      rdf:resource="http://www.linckels.lu/demo/Person" />
</rdf:Description>
```

```
<demo:Person rdf:about="http://www.linckels.lu/">
   <demo:fullname>Serge Linckels</demo:fullname>
</demo:Person>
```

Since a predicate is always a directed graph, the fact that "Serge Linckels" trains with "David Arendt" does not mean that "David Arendt" trains with "Serge Linckels". To state this information explicitly, we need to create two instances of the property **trainsWith**, one for every direction. Properties can be transitive, symmetric, inverse, or functional inverse.

Contrary to XML and XML Schema, RDF and RDF Schema are defined in the same file.

2.4.3 Complete Example

The meaning of figure 2.5 as described in section 2.3.4 could be represented by the following RDF/XML code. We suppose that **rdf**, **rdfs** and **demo** are shortened URIs as explained on page 34.

Tip: Shorter URIs

XML offers the possibility to shorten URIs by specifying an abbreviation at the beginning of the document. The following code illustrates this possibility by declaring demo as an abbreviation for the respective URI.

```
<!DOCTYPE rdf:RDF[
  <!ENTITY demo 'http://www.linckels.lu/demo/'>
]>
```

If this code is put at the very beginning of an XML document, then one can write:

```
<rdf:type rdf:resource="&demo;Person" />
```

instead of:

```
<rdf:type rdf:resource="http://www.linckels.lu/demo/Person" />
```

```
<?xml version="1.0" encoding="UTF-8"?>

<!DOCTYPE rdf:RDF[
 <!ENTITY rdf 'http://www.w3.org/1999/02/22-rdf-syntax-ns#'>
 <!ENTITY rdfs 'http://www.w3.org/2000/01/rdf-schema#'>
 <!ENTITY demo 'http://www.linckels.lu/demo/'>
]>

<rdf:RDF
  xmlns:rdf="http://www.w3.org/1999/02/22-rdf-syntax-ns#"
  xmlns:demo="http://www.linckels.lu/demo/"
  xmlns:rdfs="http://www.w3.org/2000/01/rdf-schema#">

  <rdfs:Class rdf:about="&demo;Person">
    <rdfs:subClassOf rdf:resource="&rdf;Resource" />
  </rdfs:Class>

  <rdfs:Class rdf:about="&demo;Technique">
    <rdfs:subClassOf rdf:resource="&rdf;Resource" />
  </rdfs:Class>

  <rdf:Property rdf:about="&demo;fullname">
    <rdfs:domain rdf:resource="&demo;Person" />
    <rdfs:range rdf:resource="&rdfs;string" />
  </rdf:Property>

  <rdf:Property rdf:about="&demo;trainsWith">
    <rdfs:domain rdf:resource="&demo;Person" />
    <rdfs:range rdf:resource="&demo;Person" />
  </rdf:Property>
```

```
<rdf:Property rdf:about="&demo;performs">
  <rdfs:domain rdf:resource="&demo;Person" />
  <rdfs:range rdf:resource="&demo;Technique" />
</rdf:Property>

<rdf:Property rdf:about="&demo;description">
  <rdfs:domain rdf:resource="&demo;Technique" />
  <rdfs:range rdf:resource="&rdfs;string" />
</rdf:Property>

<demo:Technique rdf:about="KICK1">
  <demo:description>yop chagi</demo:description>
</demo:Technique>

<demo:Technique rdf:about="KICK2">
  <demo:description>dollyo chagi</demo:description>
</demo:Technique>

<demo:Person rdf:about="19780329123">
  <demo:fullname>David Arendt</demo:fullname>
  <demo:trainsWith
      rdf:resource="http://www.linckels.lu/" />
  <demo:performs rdf:resource="KICK2" />
</demo:Person>

<demo:Person rdf:about="http://www.linckels.lu/">
  <demo:fullname>Serge Linckels</demo:fullname>
  <demo:trainsWith rdf:resource="19780329123" />
  <demo:performs rdf:resource="KICK1" />
</demo:Person>
</rdf:RDF>
```

2.4.4 Limitations of RDF

Although RDF is a powerful language to describe and serialize semantics in a machine readable form, it lacks expressiveness when it comes to restrictions over properties, e.g., it is not possible to specify if a person can perform only techniques or if he can also perform other things. Or, does every person have to train with at least one other person? Such information cannot be formalized with RDF.

> **Closed vs. Open World Assumption**
>
> The *open world assumption* (OWA) assumes that its knowledge of the world is incomplete. If something cannot be proven to be true, then it does not automatically become false. In the OWA, what is not stated is considered unknown, rather than wrong.
>
> In contrast to this, the *closed world assumption* (CWA) is the presumption that what is not currently known to be true is false.
>
> For illustration, consider the statement "Serge is a citizen of Luxembourg" and the question: "Is Serge a citizen of Germany?". The CWA-answer is "no", but OWA-answer is "unkown".
>
> Semantic Web languages such as RDF and OWL implicitly make the OWA. In essence, from the absence of a statement alone, a deductive reasoner cannot (and must not) infer that the statement is false.

2.5 OWL 1 and OWL 2 – Web Ontology Language

The *Web Ontology Language*[31] (OWL) has been a W3C recommendation since 2009. It is based on the idea of defining and instantiating ontologies. An OWL ontology may include descriptions of classes along with their related properties and instances. It facilitates greater machine interpretability of Web content than the content supported by XML and RDF by providing additional vocabulary along with a formal semantics. OWL introduces the following benefits:

- OWL allows to define ontologies by means of classes (concepts) that are organized in a hierarchical way and relations between classes.
- More complex relations are possible, e.g., quantified restrictions and difference operation.
- OWL 1 exists in the three levels of expressiveness Lite, DL, and Full, while OWL 2 exists in the three profiles EL, QL, and RL.
- OWL can be serialized as XML (or in other formats like *Turtle* or *Manchester Syntax*).

An ontology is defined in an OWL document with a header, e.g,

```
<owl:Ontology rdf:about="">
  <rdfs:comment>Example of an ontology</rdfs:comment>
  <owl:versionInfo>v0.5</owl:versionInfo>
  <owl:imports rdf:resource="http://www.linckels.lu/demo" />
</owl:Ontology>
```

This section gives an overview of OWL. More exhaustive explanations can be found, e.g., in [AH08, Lac05, HKR10, BCT07, AvH04].

---

[31] http://www.w3.org/TR/owl2-overview/

2.5.1 Instances, Classes and Restrictions in OWL

A class is defined in OWL with the element `owl:Class`. There are two prede-
fined classes:

- `owl:Thing`, the top class (⊤) which contains all individuals, identical to
  the RDF Schema class `rdfs:resource`,
- `owl:Nothing`, the bottom or empty class (⊥).

In OWL, properties (also called *roles*) are similar to RDF properties. In
RDF, there is only `rdf:Property` to define a property. In OWL, there are
two possibilities:

- `owl:DatatypeProperty` that defines a property with a datatype in XML
  Schema (see appendix A), e.g., `xs:integer`,
- `owl:ObjectProperty` that defines a relation between two classes.

The following example shows the definition of the property `fullname` of
the datatype `string` for the class `Person` and the property `performs` as a
relation from the class `Person` to the class `Technique`. We suppose that `xs`
and `demo` are shortened URIs as explained on page 34.

```
<owl:DatatypeProperty rdf:about="&demo;fullname">
  <rdfs:domain rdf:resource="&demo;Person" />
  <rdfs:range rdf:resource="&xs;string" />
</owl:DatatypeProperty>

<owl:ObjectProperty rdf:about="&demo;performs">
  <rdfs:domain rdf:resource="&demo;Person" />
  <rdfs:range rdf:resource="&demo;Technique" />
</owl:ObjectProperty>
```

In addition to the above RDF property definition, OWL allows to define
restrictions over properties. The following two quantifiers are possible:

- the *universal quantifier* (∀), written `allValuesFrom` to specify that the
  property can only have values from the given class, e.g., a person can only
  train with other persons,
- the *existential quantifier* (∃), written `someValuesFrom` to specify that the
  property must have at least one value from the given class, e.g., a person
  must a least perform one technique.

A more complex class definition is possible by creating an intersection
(conjunction) of different restrictions using the element `intersectionOf`. The
way the items of the intersection should be parsed can be indicated with the
attribute `parseType`. Here, `Collection` means: unordered list of items.

The following example creates the class `Person` with the restriction that
every person must perform at least one technique and can only train with
other people. We suppose that `demo` is a shortened URI, as explained on page
34.

```
<owl:Class rdf:about="&demo;Person">
  <owl:intersectionOf rdf:parseType="Collection">

    <owl:Restriction>
      <owl:onProperty rdf:resource="&demo;performs" />
      <owl:someValuesFrom rdf:resource="&demo;Technique" />
    </owl:Restriction>

    <owl:Restriction>
      <owl:onProperty rdf:resource="&demo;trainsWith" />
      <owl:allValuesFrom rdf:resource="&demo;Person" />
    </owl:Restriction>

  </owl:intersectionOf>
</owl:Class>
```

2.5.2 Complete Example

The meaning of figure 2.5, as described in section 2.3.4, could be represented by the following OWL/XML code. We suppose that rdf, rdfs and demo are shortened URIs, as explained on page 34.

```
<?xml version="1.0" encoding="UTF-8"?>

<!DOCTYPE rdf:RDF [
 <!ENTITY xs 'http://www.w3.org/2001/XMLSchema#'>
 <!ENTITY rdf 'http://www.w3.org/1999/02/22-rdf-syntax-ns#'>
 <!ENTITY owl 'http://www.w3.org/2002/07/owl#'>
 <!ENTITY demo 'http://www.linckels.lu/demo/'>
]>

<rdf:RDF
  xmlns:rdf="http://www.w3.org/1999/02/22-rdf-syntax-ns#"
  xmlns:demo="http://www.linckels.lu/demo/"
  xmlns:owl="http://www.w3.org/2002/07/owl#"
  xmlns:xs="http://www.w3.org/2001/XMLSchema#"
  xmlns:rdfs="http://www.w3.org/2000/01/rdf-schema#">

  <owl:Ontology rdf:about="http://www.linckels.lu/demo">
    <rdfs:comment>Ontology declaration</rdfs:comment>
    <owl:versionInfo>v0.5</owl:versionInfo>
    <owl:imports
      rdf:resource="http://www.linckels.lu/demo" />
    <owl:priorVersion
      rdf:resource="http://www.linckels.lu/oldDemo" />
  </owl:Ontology>
```

```
<owl:Class rdf:about="&demo;Person">
  <rdfs:subClassOf rdf:resource="&owl;Thing" />
  <owl:intersectionOf rdf:parseType="Collection">
    <owl:Restriction>
      <owl:onProperty rdf:resource="&demo;performs" />
      <owl:someValuesFrom
            rdf:resource="&demo;Technique" />
    </owl:Restriction>

    <owl:Restriction>
      <owl:onProperty rdf:resource="&demo;trainsWith" />
      <owl:allValuesFrom rdf:resource="&demo;Person" />
    </owl:Restriction>
  </owl:intersectionOf>
</owl:Class>

<owl:Class rdf:about="&demo;Technique">
  <rdfs:subClassOf rdf:resource="&owl;Thing" />
</owl:Class>

<owl:DatatypeProperty rdf:about="&demo;fullname">
  <rdfs:domain rdf:resource="&demo;Person" />
  <rdfs:range rdf:resource="&xs;string" />
</owl:DatatypeProperty>

<owl:ObjectProperty rdf:about="&demo;trainsWith">
  <rdfs:domain rdf:resource="&demo;Person" />
  <rdfs:range rdf:resource="&demo;Person" />
</owl:ObjectProperty>

<owl:ObjectProperty rdf:about="&demo;performs">
  <rdfs:domain rdf:resource="&demo;Person" />
  <rdfs:range rdf:resource="&demo;Technique" />
</owl:ObjectProperty>

<owl:DatatypeProperty rdf:about="&demo;description">
  <rdfs:domain rdf:resource="&demo;Person" />
  <rdfs:range rdf:resource="&xs;string" />
</owl:DatatypeProperty>

<demo:Technique rdf:about="KICK1">
  <demo:description>yop chagi</demo:description>
</demo:Technique>

<demo:Technique rdf:about="KICK2">
  <demo:description>dollyo chagi</demo:description>
</demo:Technique>
```

```
<demo:Person rdf:about="19780329123">
  <demo:fullname>David Arendt</demo:fullname>
  <demo:trainsWith
       rdf:resource="http://www.linckels.lu/" />
  <demo:performs rdf:resource="KICK2" />
</demo:Person>

<demo:Person rdf:about="http://www.linckels.lu/">
  <demo:fullname>Serge Linckels</demo:fullname>
  <demo:trainsWith rdf:resource="19780329123" />
  <demo:performs rdf:resource="KICK1" />
</demo:Person>
</rdf:RDF>
```

2.5.3 From OWL 1 to OWL 2

OWL has been a W3C recommendation since 2004. OWL 2, the successor of OWL 1, has been a W3C recommendation since 2009. OWL 2 has a very similar overall structure to OWL 1 and is completely backward compatible. Almost all the building blocks of OWL 2 were present in OWL 1. Also, the central role of RDF has not changed. OWL 2 adds new functionality, e.g., disjoint union of classes and new expressivity, e.g., role chains, richer datatypes, qualified cardinality restrictions, and asymmetric, reflexive and disjoint properties. OWL 2 also defines three new profiles, i.e., EL, QL, and RL.

For illustrative purposes, consider the following statement: "The brother of my father is my uncle." This could not be expressed in OWL 1. A turnaround was to use a complementary language like the *Semantic Web Rule Language*[32] (SWRL). SWRL combines OWL with the *Rule Markup Language*[33]. Rules are Horn-clauses of the form of an implication between an antecedent (*body*) and consequent (*head*). The intended meaning can be read as: whenever the conditions specified in the antecedent hold, the conditions specified in the consequent must also hold. The following code depicts the rule:

$$hasUncle(x,z) : -hasBrother(y,z), hasFather(x,y)$$

OWL 2 fixes this weakness of OWL 1 with the concept of property chains. Formally, the statement: "The brother of my father is my uncle" would result in a role concatenation like:

$$hasParent \circ hasBrother \sqsubseteq hasUncle.$$

In OWL 2/XML syntax, this would result in the following code:

---

[32] http://www.w3.org/Submission/SWRL/
[33] http://www.ruleml.org/

```
<owl:ObjectProperty rdf:about="hasUncle">
  <owl:propertyChainAxiom rdf:parseType="Collection">
    <owl:ObjectProperty rdf:about="hasParent" />
    <owl:ObjectProperty rdf:about="hasBrother" />
  </owl:propertyChainAxiom>
</owl:ObjectProperty>
```

2.5.4 SPARQL, the Query Language

SPARQL[34] is a RDF query language that stands for *SPARQL Protocol and RDF Query Language*. It has been a W3C recommendation since 2008. SPARQL allows for a query to consist of triple patterns, conjunctions, disjunctions, and optional patterns.

This section gives an overview of SPARQL. More exhaustive explanations can be found, e.g., in [AH08, HKR10, BCT07, AvH04, Vel10].

Several implementations for multiple programming languages exist. The overall structure of the language from a syntactic point of view resembles SQL with its three main blocks:

- The **SELECT** clause specifies the form in which the results are returned. Contrary to SQL, SPARQL results can be a table (SELECT), a graph (DESCRIBE / CONSTRUCT), or a boolean answer (ASK).
- The **FROM** clause specifies the sources or dataset to be queried.
- The **WHERE** clause is composed of a graph pattern in which some parts are replaced by variables. This pattern is used as a filter of the values of the dataset to be returned. Complex expressions are also allowed through the use of some algebraic operators.

The following example returns all the techniques that can be performed by a person:

```
@prefix demo: <http://www.linckels.lu/demo/>
SELECT DISTINCT ?X
FROM <http://www.linckels.lu/myRDF-file.rdf>
WHERE
{
   demo:Person demo:performs ?X .
}
```

In this example, the keyword @prefix declares the namespace prefix demo. The SELECT clause specifies that all different values for the variable ?X will be yielded. The FROM clause specifies the location of the file to be queried. The WHERE clause is always between brackets and is in this example composed of one pattern only. All triples found in the specified dataset in the FROM

---

[34] http://www.w3.org/TR/rdf-sparql-query/

clause are tested if they match this pattern. In this pattern, the subject and the resource are fixed, whereas the object can be anything. The result of this query is a table with only one column; the values of ?X.

As a second example, let us consider a more complex query to illustrate the use of filters. We suppose that every person has also a property **age** with an integer value. This query returns all the techniques that people between the ages of 31 and 40 can perform.

```
@prefix demo: <http://www.linckels.lu/demo/>
@prefix rdf: <http://www.w3.org/1999/02/22-rdf-syntax-ns#>
SELECT ?person ?technique
FROM <http://www.linckels.lu/myRDF-file.rdf>
WHERE
{
  ?person rdf:type demo:Person .
  ?person demo:performs ?technique .
  ?technique rdf:type demo:Technique
  ?person demo:age ?age .
  FILTER (?age > 30) .
  FILTER (?age <= 40) .
}
```

3

Description Logics and Reasoning

We introduced the Web Ontology Language (OWL 1 and OWL 2) in the previous chapter as a technical knowledge representation language. The logical formalism behind OWL is provided by Description Logics (DL). This chapter is an introduction to DL as a formalism for representing knowledge and for reasoning about it.

3.1 DL – Description Logics

DL denote a family of knowledge representation formalisms that allow to represent the terminological knowledge of an application domain in a structured and well-defined way [BCM$^+$03].

3.1.1 Concept Descriptions

In DL, the conceptual knowledge of an application domain is represented in terms of *concepts* (unary predicates) such as Person and Technique, and *roles* (binary predicates) such as fullname, trainsWith, and performs. Concepts denote sets of individuals and roles denote binary relations between individuals. Based on basic concept and role names, *concept descriptions* are built inductively using concept constructors like conjunction ($\sqcap$), disjunction ($\sqcup$), negation ($\neg$), universal quantifiers ($\forall$), and existential quantifier ($\exists$).

Example: the $\mathcal{AL}$-Language

The language $\mathcal{AL}$ (attributive language) is a minimal attributive language [SSS91]. The concept descriptions in $\mathcal{AL}$ are formed according to the following syntax rule:

$$
\begin{aligned}
C, D \rightarrow \;\; & A && \text{atomic concept} \\
& \top && \text{universal (top) concept} \\
& \bot && \text{bottom concept} \\
& \neg A && \text{atomic negation} \\
& \sqcap && \text{conjunction} \\
& \forall R.C && \text{value restriction} \\
& \exists R.\top && \text{limited existential quantification}
\end{aligned}
$$

In that abstract notation, A denotes an atomic concepts, R denotes an atomic role, and C and D denote concept descriptions.

Examples $\mathcal{AL}$-concept description:

- Person $\sqcap$ $\forall$trainsWith.Person
  a person who trains only with other people
- Person $\sqcap$ $\forall$trainsWith.(Person $\sqcap$ $\forall$perform.Technique)
  a person who trains only with people who perform only techniques
- Person $\sqcap$ $\forall$trainsWith.$\neg$Person
  a person who does not train with people

3.1.2 DL Languages

The different DL languages distinguish themselves by the kind of constructs they allow. A non-exhaustive overview of frame based languages ($\mathcal{FL}$) and attributive languages ($\mathcal{AL}$) is shown in the following table:

	A	$\top$	$\bot$	$\neg A$	$C \sqcap D$	$C \sqcup D$	$\neg C$	$\forall R.C$	$\exists R.\top$	$\exists R.C$	$\geq nR$	$\leq nR$	$= nR$
$\mathcal{ALN}$	×	×	×	×	×	×		×	×		×	×	×
$\mathcal{ALC}$	×	×	×	×	×	×	×	×	×				
$\mathcal{ALU}$	×	×	×	×	×	×		×	×				
$\mathcal{ALE}$	×	×	×	×	×			×	×	×			
$\mathcal{AL}$	×	×	×	×	×			×	×				
$\mathcal{FL}^{-}$	×	×			×			×	×				
$\mathcal{FL}_{\bot}$	×	×	×		×			×					
$\mathcal{FL}_{0}$	×	×			×			×					
$\mathcal{EL}$	×	×			×				×	×			
$\mathcal{L}$	×	×			×								

Examples of using quantifiers:

- Person $\sqcap$ $\exists$performs.Technique
  a person who performs at least one technique
- Person $\sqcap$ $\forall$performs.Technique
  a person who can only perform techniques
- Person $\sqcap$ $\forall$performs.$\top$
  a person who can perform everything

- Person $\sqcap$ $\forall$performs.$\perp$
  a person who performs nothing
- Person $\sqcap$ $\exists$performs.$\top$
  a person who performs something
- Person $\sqcap$ $\exists$performs.$\perp$
  a person who performs at least nothing (inconsistent statement)
- Person $\sqcap$ $\exists$performs.Technique $\sqcap$ $\forall$performs.Technique
  a person who performs techniques (one or more techniques and only techniques)

3.1.3 Equivalences between OWL and DL

The formal semantics of OWL are based on DL. As an example, the following DL-concept description can be written as OWL/XML (see section 2.5):

$$\text{Actor} \equiv \text{Person} \sqcap \exists\text{performs.Technique.}$$

```
<owl:Class rdf:about="&demo;Actor">
  <owl:intersectionOf rdf:parseType="Collection">
    <owl:Class rdf:about="&demo;Person" />
    <owl:Restriction>
      <owl:onProperty rdf:resource="&demo;performs" />
      <owl:someValuesFrom rdf:resource="&demo;Technique" />
    </owl:Restriction>
  </owl:intersectionOf>
</owl:Class>
```

The following table shows some equivalences between OWL and DL:

DL syntax	OWL syntax
$\top$	`<owl:Thing />`
$\perp$	`<owl:Nothing />`
C	`<owl:Class rdf:about="C" />`
R	`<owl:ObjectProperty rdf:about="R" />`
$\sqsubseteq$	`<rdfs:subClassOf />`
$\sqcap$	`<owl:intersectionOf />`
$\sqcup$	`<owl:unionOf />`
$\exists$	`<owl:someValuesFrom />`
$\forall$	`<owl:allValuesFrom />`
$\equiv$	`<owl:equivalentClass />`
$\neg$	`<owl:disjointWith />`
$\geq$	`<owl:minCardinality />`
$\leq$	`<owl:maxCardinality />`
$=$	`<owl:cardinality />`

The following table summarizes the equivalences between the OWL 1 sublanguages, OWL 2, and DL:

OWL profile	DL sub-language
OWL 1 Lite	$\mathcal{SHIF}(D)$, a subset of OWL DL
OWL 1 DL	$\mathcal{SHOIN}(D)$
OWL 1 Full	operates outside the bounds of DL
OWL 2 (general)	$\mathcal{SROIQ}(D)$
OWL 2 EL	$\mathcal{EL}^{++}(D)$

The DL sub-languages are defined as follows:

$\mathcal{F} \rightarrow$ qualified role functionality, e.g., performs.Technique

$\mathcal{E} \rightarrow$ use of existential role restriction, e.g., $\exists$performs

$\mathcal{U} \rightarrow$ use of union operator, e.g., Kick $\sqcup$ Punch

$\mathcal{S} \rightarrow \mathcal{ALC}$ plus transitive roles

$\mathcal{H} \rightarrow$ role hierarchy, e.g., performsKick $\sqsubseteq$ performs

$\mathcal{R} \rightarrow$ generalized role inclusion axioms, i.e., (ir)reflexivity and disjointness

$\mathcal{O} \rightarrow$ nominals/singleton classes, i.e., classes of object value restriction

$\mathcal{I} \rightarrow$ inverse roles, e.g., performedBy $\equiv$ performs^{-}

$\mathcal{N} \rightarrow$ cardinality restrictions, e.g., $\geq$ 2performs.Technique

$\mathcal{Q} \rightarrow$ qualified cardinality restrictions that have fillers other than $\top$

D $\rightarrow$ a datatype theory D, e.g., "1"$^{\wedge\wedge}$xs:integer.

3.2 DL Knowledge Base

A DL-knowledge base is composed of a *TBox* and an *ABox*. The TBox introduces the terminology, i.e., the vocabulary of an application domain, while the ABox contains assertions about named individuals in terms of this vocabulary.

3.2.1 Terminologies (TBox)

The first component of a DL knowledge base is *terminologies* (TBox or $\mathcal{T}$), which make statements about how concepts and roles are related to each other. Terminologies are composed of terminological axioms which can be *definitions* and *inclusion assertions*.

Definitions

Definitions allow to give a meaningful name (*concept name* or *symbolic name*) to concept descriptions. For example, to define that an actor is a person who performs at least one technique, one can write:

$$\text{Actor} \equiv \text{Person} \sqcap \exists\text{performs}.\text{Technique}.$$

Here, Actor is the concept name (or symbolic name) that identifies the concept description (on the right-hand side of the equivalent symbol). Hence, Actor is a *defined concept* by opposition to Person and Technique, which are *atomic concepts*; the latter never appear on the left-hand side of a definition.

Inclusion Assertions

Inclusion assertions express that one concept (left-hand side) is a specialization of another concept (right-hand side), i.e., that one is a subclass of the other. The following example expresses that an actor is, among other things, a kind of person:

$$\text{Actor} \sqsubseteq \text{Person}.$$

An inclusion assertion can be transformed into a definition by showing the qualities that have not been defined. The above example would become:

$$\text{Actor} \equiv \text{Person} \sqcap \overline{\text{Actor}}$$

where $\overline{\text{Actor}}$ stands for all the qualities that distinguish Actor from Person.

Cyclic and Acyclic Terminologies

A terminology is *cyclic* when its axioms (i.e., definitions and inclusion assertions) are cyclic. An axiom is cyclic when it uses itself, that means if the defined concept appears (directly or indirectly) in its own conception description. A terminology that does not contain cyclic axioms is called *acyclic*. An example of a cyclic definition is the following:

$$\text{Actor} \equiv \text{Person} \sqcap \exists \text{trainsWith.Actor}.$$

Expanding Terminologies

A terminology that is acyclic can be *expanded*. This can be done through an iterative process over the axioms by replacing each occurrence of a defined concept (on the right-hand side of the concept description) with the concepts that it stands for. Since there is no cycle in the set of definitions, the process eventually stops and the result is a terminology consisting of definitions containing only atomic concepts and no defined concepts.

Here is an example of an acyclic terminology using the atomic concepts Kick, Punch, and Person, as well as the atomic role performs, in order to define the concepts Technique and Actor.

$$\begin{aligned}
\text{Technique} &\equiv \text{Kick} \sqcup \text{Punch} \\
\text{Actor} &\equiv \text{Person} \sqcap \exists \text{performs.Technique}
\end{aligned}$$

The expansion of the above terminology would result in:

$$\begin{aligned}
\text{Technique} &\equiv \text{Kick} \sqcup \text{Punch} \\
\text{Actor} &\equiv \text{Person} \sqcap \exists \text{performs.(Kick} \sqcup \text{Punch)}
\end{aligned}$$

3.2.2 World Descriptions (ABox)

The second component of a DL-knowledge base is the world description (ABox or $\mathcal{A}$). In the ABox, one introduces individuals by giving them names and one asserts properties of these individuals. There are two kinds of assertions: *concept assertions* and *role assertions*.

Through a concept assertion, one states that an individual a belongs to a concept C, written $C(a)$. Through a role assertion, one states that an individual c is a filler of a role R for an individual b, written $R(b, c)$.

The following example of an ABox defines the person SergeLinckels with the name "Serge Linckels", the technique KICK1 with the description "Yop Chagi", and the fact that the individual SergeLinckels performs the technique YopChagi.

```
Person(SergeLinckels)
Technique(YopChagi)
fullname(SergeLinckels,"Serge Linckels")
description(YopChagi,"Yop Chagi")
performs(SergeLinckels,YopChagi)
```

The first two are concept assertions and the last three are role assertions.

3.3 Interpretations

A DL knowledge base (TBox and ABox) defines a terminology and facts of the world. To clearly define the semantics of such a knowledge base, we consider *interpretations* and *models* of the real world.

3.3.1 Interpreting Individuals, Concepts, and Roles

Formally, an interpretation $\mathcal{I}$ consists of a non-empty set $\Delta^{\mathcal{I}}$ (the domain of the interpretation) and an interpretation function $\cdot^{\mathcal{I}}$. An interpretation is written: $\mathcal{I} = (\Delta^{\mathcal{I}}, \cdot^{\mathcal{I}})$.

First, the *domain of interpretation* $\Delta^{\mathcal{I}}$ consists of all the elements that can be used in the interpretation. Note that it is important that this set not be empty. If empty domains were allowed, some important expressions would not hold, e.g., $\exists$performs.Technique because here, at least one filler for this role is required due to the existential quantifier ($\exists$). An example of a domain of interpretation is:

$$\Delta^{\mathcal{I}} = \{Serge, Yop\}.$$

Secondly, the *interpretation function* $\cdot^{\mathcal{I}}$ maps names to the domain of interpretation as follows:

- individual names I to elements of the domain, $I^{\mathcal{I}} \to \Delta^{\mathcal{I}}$
  For example: $\mathsf{SergeLinckels}^{\mathcal{I}} = Serge$
  $\qquad\qquad\quad \mathsf{YopChagi}^{\mathcal{I}} = Yop$
- concept names C to sets of elements of the domain, $C^{\mathcal{I}} \to 2^{\Delta^{\mathcal{I}}}$
  For example: $\mathsf{Person}^{\mathcal{I}} = \{Serge\}$
  $\qquad\qquad\quad \mathsf{Technique}^{\mathcal{I}} = \{Yop\}$
- role names R to sets of binary relations of the domain, $R^{\mathcal{I}} \to 2^{\Delta^{\mathcal{I}} \times \Delta^{\mathcal{I}}}$
  For example: $\mathsf{performs}^{\mathcal{I}} = \{(Serge, Yop)\}$

The interpretation function is extended to concept descriptions by the following inductive definitions (non-exhaustive list), where C and D are concepts and R is a role:

$$\top^{\mathcal{I}} = \Delta^{\mathcal{I}}$$
$$\bot^{\mathcal{I}} = \emptyset$$
$$(\neg C)^{\mathcal{I}} = \Delta^{\mathcal{I}} \setminus C^{\mathcal{I}}$$
$$(C \sqcap D)^{\mathcal{I}} = C^{\mathcal{I}} \cap D^{\mathcal{I}}$$
$$(C \sqcup D)^{\mathcal{I}} = C^{\mathcal{I}} \cup D^{\mathcal{I}}$$
$$(\forall R.C)^{\mathcal{I}} = \{x \in \Delta^{\mathcal{I}} \mid \forall y : (x,y) \in R^{\mathcal{I}} \to y \in C^{\mathcal{I}}\}$$
$$(\exists R.C)^{\mathcal{I}} = \{x \in \Delta^{\mathcal{I}} \mid \exists y : (x,y) \in R^{\mathcal{I}} \land y \in C^{\mathcal{I}}\}$$
$$(\exists R.\top)^{\mathcal{I}} = \{x \in \Delta^{\mathcal{I}} \mid \exists y : (x,y) \in R^{\mathcal{I}}\}$$

3.3.2 Modeling the Real World

Interpretations that are meaningful according to the knowledge base are called *models* and denoted $\mathcal{I} \models$. For example, consider the two interpretations performs(SergeLinckels, YopChagi)$^{\mathcal{I}}$ and performs(SergeLinckels, Tango)$^{\mathcal{I}}$. It can be verified in the above knowledge base that the first assertion holds, but not the second. In model theory we say that for the first case, $\mathcal{I}$ is a model, but not for the second case. Formally,

- $\mathcal{I} \models$ performs(SergeLinckels, YopChagi)
  because performs(SergeLinckels, YopChagi)$^{\mathcal{I}} \neq \emptyset$,
- $\mathcal{I} \not\models$ performs(SergeLinckels, Tango)
  because performs(SergeLinckels, Tango)$^{\mathcal{I}} = \emptyset$.

Consistency of a DL Knowledge Base

If $\mathcal{I}$ is a model for all representations in the knowledge base, then we say that the interpretation models the knowledge base, written $\mathcal{I} \models K$, where K is a knowledge base. In that case, the following constraints must hold (non-exhaustive list):

- for all $C(a) \in K$ holds: $a^{\mathcal{I}} \in C^{\mathcal{I}}$

  For example: Person(SergeLinckels) holds for SergeLinckels$^{\mathcal{I}} \in$ Person$^{\mathcal{I}}$
  Proof: SergeLinckels$^{\mathcal{I}} = Serge$ and
  Person$^{\mathcal{I}} = \{Serge\}$ and
  $Serge \in \{Serge\}$.

- for all $R(a,b) \in K$ holds: $(a^{\mathcal{I}}, b^{\mathcal{I}}) \in R^{\mathcal{I}}$

  For example: performs(SergeLinckels, YopChagi) holds for
  (SergeLinckels$^{\mathcal{I}}$, YopChagi$^{\mathcal{I}}$) $\in$ performs$^{\mathcal{I}}$
  Proof: SergeLinckels$^{\mathcal{I}} = Serge$ and
  YopChagi$^{\mathcal{I}} = Yop$ and
  performs$^{\mathcal{I}} = \{(Serge, Yop)\}$ and
  $(Serge, Yop) \in \{(Serge, Yop)\}$.

- for all $C \sqsubseteq D \in K$ holds: $C^{\mathcal{I}} \subseteq D^{\mathcal{I}}$

  For example: Actor $\sqsubseteq$ Person holds for Actor$^{\mathcal{I}} \subseteq$ Person$^{\mathcal{I}}$
  Proof: Actor$^{\mathcal{I}} = \{Serge\}$ and
  Person$^{\mathcal{I}} = \{Serge\}$ and
  $\{Serge\} \subseteq \{Serge\}$.

A model provides a meaningful view of the knowledge base and captures its structure. However, different models are possible. Let us consider the following interpretations:

	Model 1 $(M1)$	Model 2 $(M2)$	Model 3 $(M3)$
$\Delta^{\mathcal{I}}$	$\{Serge, David\}$	$\{toto, titi, tutu\}$	$\{x\}$
SergeLinckels$^{\mathcal{I}}$	$Serge$	$toto$	x
DavidArendt$^{\mathcal{I}}$	$David$	$titi$	x
Person(SergeLinckels)$^{\mathcal{I}}$	$\{Serge\}$	$\{tutu\}$	$\{x\}$
Person$^{\mathcal{I}}$	$\{Serge, David\}$	$\{toto, titi\}$	$\{x, x\}$
therefore:	$\mathcal{I}^{M1} \models K$	$\mathcal{I}^{M2} \not\models K$	$\mathcal{I}^{M3} \models K$

Remarks:

- Model 1 provides a valid view of the knowledge base because $\mathcal{I}$ is a model for all representations, therefore $\mathcal{I}^{M1} \models K$.
- Model 2 does not provide a valid view of the knowledge base because SergeLinckels$^{\mathcal{I}} \notin$ Person(SergeLinckels)$^{\mathcal{I}}$, therefore $\mathcal{I}^{M2} \not\models K$.
- Model 3 is correct in terms of model theory, but in OWL, we assume that different individual names state different elements. However, in this example, SergeLinckels$^{\mathcal{I}} =$ DavidArendt$^{\mathcal{I}}$.

A knowledge base is called *consistent* or *satisfiable*, written $K \models$, if it has at least one model, otherwise it is *inconsistent*, written $K \not\models$. For example, the knowledge base described above is consistent because it has two models, i.e., model 1 and model 3.

Logical Consequence

Let α be an inclusion assertion of the form $C \sqsubseteq D$, a concept assignment of the form $C(a)$ or a role assignment of the form $R(a, b)$. Therefore, α is a *logical consequence* of the knowledge base K, written $K \models \alpha$, if $a^{\mathcal{I}}$ holds for every model of K.

As a first example, let us consider Person, which is a logical consequence of the knowledge base shown above, because $\text{Person}^{\mathcal{I}}$ holds for all three models M_1, M_2, and M_3. We write: $K \models \text{Person}$, because for all three models, $\mathcal{I} \models$ Person holds and we say that Person is a logical consequence of the knowledge base.

Proof:

	Model 1	Model 2	Model 3
$\text{Person}^{\mathcal{I}}$	$\{Serge, David\}$	$\{toto, titi\}$	$\{x, x\}$
$\text{SergeLinckels}^{\mathcal{I}}$	$Serge$	$toto$	x
$\text{DavidArendt}^{\mathcal{I}}$	$David$	$titi$	x
then:	$David \in \{Serge, David\}$	$titi \in \{toto, titi\}$	$x \in \{x\}$
	$Serge \in \{Serge, David\}$	$toto \in \{toto, titi\}$	$x \in \{x\}$
therefore:	$\mathcal{I}^{M1} \models \text{Person}$	$\mathcal{I}^{M2} \models \text{Person}$	$\mathcal{I}^{M3} \models \text{Person}$

As a second example, let us consider Person(SergeLinckels), which is not a logical consequence of the knowledge base. The reason for this is that $\text{Person(SergeLinckels)}^{\mathcal{I}}$ does not hold for model 2. Therefore, this assertion is not a model of the knowledge base. We write: $K \not\models \text{Person(SergeLinckels)}$, because $\mathcal{I} \models \text{Person(SergeLinckels)}$ holds for model 1 and model 3, but not for model 2.

Proof:

	Model 1	Model 2	Model 3
$\text{Person(SergeLinckels)}^{\mathcal{I}}$	$\{Serge\}$	$\{tutu\}$	$\{x\}$
$\text{SergeLinckels}^{\mathcal{I}}$	$Serge$	$toto$	x
then:	$Serge \in \{Serge\}$	$toto \notin \{tutu\}$	$x \in \{x\}$
therefore:	$\mathcal{I}^{M1} \models \text{Person}$	$\mathcal{I}^{M2} \not\models \text{Person}$	$\mathcal{I}^{M3} \models \text{Person}$

3.4 Inferences

The main feature of DL and DL-based knowledge representation systems are inference services, which allow to derive implicit knowledge from the knowledge that is explicitly stored in the knowledge base. We will give here an overview of the most important ones, typically divided into standard- and non-standard inferences.

3.4.1 Standard Inferences

"Classical" reasoning services are called *standard inferences*. In this section, we explain the most important ones: concept satisfiability, subsumption, equivalence/disjointess, instance checking, and consistency check.

Satisfiability (concepts)

In classical logics like propositional logic, expressions are *true* (1) or *false* (0). For example, p stands for "he performs a technique" and a stands for "he is an actor", then the formula $p \rightarrow a$ is true if p and a are true, or if p is false, as demonstrated in the following truth table. The expression $p \rightarrow a$ says that if he performs a technique, then he is an actor.

p	a	$p \rightarrow a$
0	0	1
0	1	1
1	0	0
1	1	1

DL is not about true or false, but about *satisfiability*. Testing if a concept or role is satisfiable means, testing if its interpretation is not an empty set (see section 3.3).

For example, the concept Person is satisfiable if $\mathsf{Person}^{\mathcal{I}} \neq \emptyset$, i.e., if $\mathcal{I} \models$ Person. In the above knowledge base, we have defined a model M1 for which $\mathsf{Person}^{\mathcal{I}} = \{Serge, David\}$. Therefore, Person is satisfiable in $\mathcal{I}^{M1}$.

Checking satisfiability of concepts is a key inference. A number of other important inferences can be reduced to (un)satisfiability.

Subsumption (concepts)

Subsumption allows to compute sub- and super-concept relationships. For example, Actor $\sqsubseteq$ Person means that the concept Person (the *subsumer*) is more general than the concept Actor (the *subsumee*). One says: "Actor is subsumed by Person" or "Person subsumes Actor". Formally, Actor $\sqsubseteq$ Person if $\mathsf{Actor}^{\mathcal{I}} \subseteq \mathsf{Person}^{\mathcal{I}}$ for all interpretations $\mathcal{I}$.

As already stated above, all standard reasoning tasks can be reduced to satisfiability. For DLs that allow full negation like $\mathcal{ALC}$, subsumption can be reduced to unsatisfiability since:

$$\mathsf{Actor} \sqsubseteq \mathsf{Person} \text{ iff } (\mathsf{Actor} \sqcap \neg\mathsf{Person} \equiv \bot).$$

Also, satisfiability can be reduced to subsumption since Actor is satisfiable in $\mathcal{I}$ if Actor $\not\sqsubseteq \bot$ or Actor $\equiv \bot$.

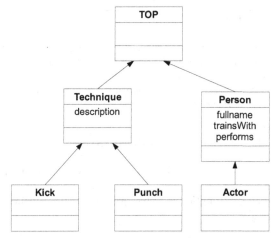

Fig. 3.1. Class hierarchy (taxonomy) using the UML formalism.

Equivalence and Disjointness (concepts)

Two concepts can have different names but represent the same meaning, e.g., the English word "actor" and the French word "acteur". The equivalence between the two concepts Actor and Acteur is written Actor $\equiv$ Acteur, if $\text{Actor}^{\mathcal{I}} = \text{Acteur}^{\mathcal{I}}$ for all interpretations $\mathcal{I}$. In the same sense, two concepts are disjoint, written Actor $\not\equiv$ Acteur, if $\text{Actor}^{\mathcal{I}} \cap \text{Acteur}^{\mathcal{I}} = \emptyset$ for all interpretations $\mathcal{I}$.

Testing equivalence can be reduced to subsumption checking because:

$$\text{Actor} \equiv \text{Acteur iff (Actor} \sqsubseteq \text{Acteur and Acteur} \sqsubseteq \text{Actor}).$$

Also, subsumption can be reduced to equivalence checking since:

$$\text{Actor} \sqsubseteq \text{Person iff (Actor} \equiv \text{Actor} \sqcap \text{Person}).$$

Instance Checking (ABox)

An individual SergeLinckels is an instance of a concept Actor if Actor(SergeLinckels) is a logical consequence of the ABox, written $\mathcal{A} \models$ Actor(SergeLinckels). As explained in section 3.3, $\mathcal{A} \models$ Actor(SergeLinckels) if Actor(SergeLinckels)$^{\mathcal{I}} \neq \emptyset$.

Instance checking can be used to derive *implicit knowledge* from a knowledge base. Let us consider the following knowledge base:

> Actor $\equiv$ Person $\sqcap$ $\exists$performs. Technique
>
> Person(SergeLinckels)
> Technique(YopChagi)
> performs(SergeLinckels, YopChagi)

Reasoning over a TBox

In a DL system, usually all concepts are well defined in a TBox. To state explicitly that a reasoning task is performed with respect to a TBox we write: $C \sqsubseteq_{\mathcal{T}} D$, where $\mathcal{T}$ specifies the TBox.

For illustration, suppose the following TBox that is composed only of one inclusion assertion: $\mathcal{T} = \{\mathsf{Actor} \sqsubseteq \mathsf{Person}\}$. As a result:

- Actor $\sqsubseteq_{\mathcal{T}}^{?}$ Person
  holds because the subsumption is tested with respect to $\mathcal{T}$,
- Actor $\sqsubseteq^{?}$ Person
  does not hold because the subsumption is tested over an empty TBox,
- Actor $\sqcap$ Person $\sqsubseteq^{?}$ Person
  holds because the subsumption is tested over an extended inclusion assertion.

Explanation:

Remember that subsumption states that the expression on the left-hand side is more specific than the expression on the right-hand side. If the subsumption check is done over an empty TBox, e.g., Actor $\sqsubseteq^{?}$ Person, then the expression on the left-hand side must contain every concept that exists on the right-hand side. If the subsumption check is done over a non-empty TBox, e.g., Actor $\sqsubseteq_{\mathcal{T}}^{?}$ Person, then the reasoning task is performed with respect to the indicated TBox, i.e., with the knowledge that Actor $\sqsubseteq$ Person.

The first line is a TBox definition and the next three lines are ABox assertions. The knowledge base states that: *An actor is a person who performs at least one technique. Serge Linckels is a person. He performs the technique "yop chagi".*

We never asserted that Serge Linckels is an actor. But by logical reasoning, a DL system can come to the conclusion that the knowledge base entails the information that Serge Linckels is an actor. Formally,

$$\mathcal{I} \models \mathsf{Actor}(\mathsf{Serge\ Linckels}) \text{ because } \mathsf{Actor}(\mathsf{Serge\ Linckels})^{\mathcal{I}} \neq \emptyset.$$

Proof:

In a model-theoretic view, the above ABox results in:

$$
\begin{array}{l}
\Delta^{\mathcal{I}} = \{Serge, Yop\} \\
\mathsf{Person}^{\mathcal{I}} = \{Serge, David\} \\
\mathsf{Technique}^{\mathcal{I}} = \{Yop\} \\
\mathsf{performs}^{\mathcal{I}} = \{(Serge, Yop)\}
\end{array}
$$

With respect to the mapping rules explained in section 3.3.1, we get:

Actor(SergeLinckels)$^{\mathcal{I}}$

$$= \text{Person}^{\mathcal{I}} \cap \{x \in \Delta^{\mathcal{I}} \mid \exists y : (x,y) \in \text{performs}^{\mathcal{I}} \wedge y \in \text{Technique}^{\mathcal{I}}\}$$
$$= \{Serge\} \cap \{x \in \Delta^{\mathcal{I}} \mid \exists y : (x,y) \in \{(Serge, Yop)\} \wedge y \in \{Yop\}\}$$
$$= \{Serge\} \cap \{Serge \mid Yop \wedge Yop\}$$
$$= \{Serge\} \cap \{Serge\}$$
$$= \{Serge\}$$

Actor(SergeLinckels)$^{\mathcal{I}} = \{Serge\}$

therefore: $\mathcal{I} \models$ Actor(SergeLinckels).

Instance checking can be reduced to consistency. If $\mathcal{A} \models$ Actor(SergeLinckels), then $\mathcal{A} \cup \{\neg\text{Actor(SergeLinckels)}\}$ must be inconsistent.

An extended form of instance checking is the so called *retrieval problem*. It is stated as follows: given an ABox $\mathcal{A}$ and a concept Actor, find all individuals x such that $\mathcal{A} \models$ Actor(x).

Consistency check (ABox)

An ABox $\mathcal{A}$ is consistent (written $\mathcal{A} \not\models$) if no assertion is contradictory to the TBox. In other words, all assertions can be satisfiable simultaneously. In terms of interpretations, an ABox is consistent if it has at least one model (see section 3.3). For illustration, consider the following TBox:

Actor $\equiv$ Person $\sqsubseteq \exists$performs.Technique
Actor $\sqsubseteq$ Person
Person $\equiv \neg$Technique

The assertions Actor(SergeLinckels) and Technique(SergeLinckels) would result in an inconsistent ABox, because the actor SergeLinckels, which is by logical inference also a person, cannot be an instance of the concept Technique at the same time.

3.4.2 Non-Standard Inferences

Beside the "classical" standard inferences, new reasoning services have been introduced. Those supplementary and complementary inferences are called *non-standard inferences*. In this section, we explain the following ones: most specific concept, least common subsumer, difference operation, concept matching, concept rewriting, concept cover, concept contraction, and concept abduction

Most Specific Concept (ABox)

The most specific concept of individuals is a concept description that represents all the properties of the individuals including the concept assertions in which they occur and their relationship to other individuals [Neb90].

| Kick ⊑ Technique |
| Punch ⊑ Technique |
| Actor ≡ Person ⊓ ∃performs.Technique |
| Person ≡ ¬Technique |

TBox ($\mathcal{T}$)

| Actor(Serge) |
| Actor(David) |
| Kick(Yopchagi) |
| Punch(MomtongJirugi) |

ABox ($\mathcal{A}$)

Fig. 3.2. Example of a TBox and an ABox

Definition 3.1 (most specific concept). *Let $\mathcal{A}$ be an ABox and $a_1, ..., a_k$ be individuals of $\mathcal{A}$. C is a most specific concept (msc) of $a_1, ..., a_k$ iff:*

- $\mathcal{A} \models C(a_i), i \in [1..k]$ *and*
- *C is the most specific concept with this property, i.e., for all concept descriptions D, if $\mathcal{A} \models D(a_i), i \in [1..k]$, then $C \sqsubseteq D$.*

Examples:

Consider the TBox and ABox shown in figure 3.2, then:
   msc(YopChagi, MomtongJirugi) = Technique
   msc(Serge, David) = Actor
   msc(Serge, Yopchagi) = ⊤

Least Common Subsumer (concepts)

The least common subsumer (lcs) stands for the least concept description that subsumes a given set of concept descriptions [BKM99].

Definition 3.2 (least common subsumer). *Let $C_1, ..., C_k$ be concept descriptions. The concept description C is a least common subsumer (lcs) of $C_1, ..., C_k$ iff:*

- $C_i \sqsubseteq C, i \in [1..k]$ *and*
- *C is the most specific concept with this property, i.e., for every concept description E, if $C_i \sqsubseteq E, i \in [1..k]$, then $C \sqsubseteq E$.*

Examples:

Consider the TBox and ABox shown in figure 3.2, then:
   lcs(Kick, Punch) = Technique
   lcs(Person, Actor) = Person
   lcs(Person, Technique) = ⊤
   lcs(Person, Person ⊓ Technique) = Person

Difference Operation

The difference operation allows to remove from a given concept description all the information contained in another concept description [Tee94].

Definition 3.3 (semantic difference). *Let C and D be two concept descriptions with $C \sqsubseteq D$. The difference is defined by:*

$$C - D := \max_{\sqsubseteq}\{B | B \sqcap D \equiv C\}.$$

First, every description B in the result contains enough information to yield the information in C if added to D, i.e., it contains every piece of information from C which is missing in D. Secondly, B is maximally general, i.e., it does not contain any additional unnecessary information.

Examples:

Consider the TBox and ABox shown in figure 3.2, then:

- Actor - Person $=$ ∃performs.Technique
- Person - Actor $=$ not possible because Person $\not\sqsubseteq$ Actor
- Actor - Actor $=$ ⊤
- Actor - ⊤ $=$ Actor because Actor $\sqcap$ ⊤ $=$ Actor
- Actor - ∃performs.⊤ $=$ Actor
- Actor - ∃performs.Technique $=$ Person
- Actor - Technique $=$ not possible because Actor $\not\sqsubseteq$ Technique

The above definition of semantic difference requires that the second argument subsumes the first one. However, the semantic difference between two incomparable descriptions can be given by computing the least common subsumer, e.g.,

$$C - D = C - lcs(C, D).$$

Examples:

Consider the TBox and ABox shown in figure 3.2. As a result:

-
  Actor - Technique $=$ Actor - lcs(Actor,Technique)
  $\qquad\qquad\qquad = $ Actor - ⊤
  $\qquad\qquad\qquad = $ Actor

-
  Person - Actor $=$ Person - lcs(Person,Actor)
  $\qquad\qquad\qquad = $ Person - Person
  $\qquad\qquad\qquad = $ ⊤

-
  Kick - Punch $=$ Kick - lcs(Kick,Punch)
  $\qquad\qquad\quad = $ Kick - Technique
  $\qquad\qquad\quad = $ Kick

Another definition of difference operator is the *syntactic difference* [BKT02]. Here, the minimum with respect to $\prec_d$ is used instead of the maximum with respect to a syntactic order $\sqsubseteq$.

Matching of Concept Descriptions (concepts)

Matching is an inference service that allows to replace certain concept names by concept descriptions before one can test for equivalence or subsumption [Küs01, Bra06].

Definition 3.4 (matching). *A matching problem modulo equivalence and modulo subsumption is of the form $C \equiv^? D$ and $C \sqsubseteq^? D$ respectively, where C is a description and D a pattern. A solution or matcher of these problems is a substitution $\mathcal{A}$ such that $C \equiv \mathcal{A}(D)$ and $C \sqsubseteq \mathcal{A}(D)$, respectively.*

Example:

Consider the TBox and ABox shown in figure 3.2. As a result:
    Let P be a pattern such that

$$P : X \sqcap \exists \mathsf{performs}.Y$$

where X and Y are concept variables. P matches against Actor when replacing X by Person and Y by Technique, because:

$$\mathsf{Actor} \equiv \mathsf{Person} \sqcap \exists \mathsf{performs}.\mathsf{Technique}.$$

Concept Rewriting (concepts)

Given a concept expressed in a source language, concept rewriting aims to find a concept expressed in a target language, which is related to the given concept according to equivalence, subsumption, or some other relation [BKM00]. Concept rewriting can be applied to the translation of concepts from one knowledge base to another, or in the reformulation of concepts during the process of knowledge base construction and maintenance.

Definition 3.5 (rewriting). *Let N_r be a set of role names and N_p a set of primitive concept names and let $\mathcal{L}_s, \mathcal{L}_d$ and $\mathcal{L}_t$ be three DLs (the source-, destination, and TBox, respectively). A rewriting problem is given by:*

- *an $\mathcal{L}_t$-TBox $\mathcal{T}$ containing only role names from N_r and primitive names from N_p,*
- *an $\mathcal{L}_s$-concept description C using only the names from N_r and N_p.*

A rewriting of C using $\mathcal{T}$ is an $\mathcal{L}_d$-concept description D which is built using names from N_r and $N_p \cup N_p$ such that C and D are equivalent modulo $\mathcal{T}$.

Example:

Let us suppose that:

> $\mathcal{T}$ = the TBox show in figure 3.2
> $C \equiv \exists \text{performs.}(\text{Kick} \sqcup \text{Punch})$

As a result:

> $D \equiv \exists \text{performs.Technique}$

Here, D is the rewriting of C using the TBox $\mathcal{T}$. It is specified in $\mathcal{T}$ that Kick $\sqsubseteq$ Technique and Punch $\sqsubseteq$ Technique, therefore, Technique $\equiv$ Kick $\sqcup$ Punch.

Concept Cover (concepts)

The concept covering problem defines a cover of a concept description C as being the conjunction of some concepts used in a terminology [HLRT02]. Based on two non-standard inferences, i.e., the least common subsumer and the semantic difference, a cover can be formally defined as follows:

Definition 3.6 (concept cover). *Let $S_\mathcal{T} = \{S_i, i \in [1, n]\}$ be the set of concept definitions occurring in the TBox $\mathcal{T}$. A cover of a concept description $C \not\equiv \bot$ with respect to $\mathcal{T}$ is a conjunction E of some names S_i from $\mathcal{T}$ such that $C - lcs(C, E) \not\equiv C$.*

Example

Let $C \equiv A_1 \sqcap A_2 \sqcap A_3 \sqcap A_4$ and the following terminology:

$$D_1 \equiv A_1 \sqcap A_2$$
$$D_2 \equiv A_2 \sqcap A_3$$
$$D_3 \equiv A_2 \sqcap A_3 \sqcap A_4$$
$$D_4 \equiv A_1$$

The aim is to find the optimal conjunctions of defined concepts (D_1 to D_4) that cover C. A *best cover* is a conjunction that contains all concepts from C.

	A_1	A_2	A_3	A_4
D_1	×	×		
D_2		×	×	
D_3		×	×	×
D_4	×			

As depicted in the above table, best covers are: $D_3 \sqcap D_4$ and $D_1 \sqcap D_3$. Both contain all concepts used in C, i.e., $A_1 \sqcap A_2 \sqcap A_3 \sqcap A_4$.

A new definition of the concept covering problem is given in section 8.1.3.

Concept Contraction and Concept Abduction

Concept contraction and concept abduction are two inference services that were introduced as a solution to find an optimal equilibrium between a demand (D) and a supply (S) [CNS$^+$05, CNS$^+$03]. The algorithm was implemented in a project for semantic-based discovery of matches and negotiation spaces in an e-marketplace.

Concept contraction extends satisfiability. If the conjunction between the supply and the demand is unsatisfiable in the TBox $\mathcal{T}$, written $S \sqcap D \equiv_{\mathcal{T}} \bot$, then the aim is to retract requirements in D to obtain a concept K (for keep) such that $K \sqcap S \not\equiv_{\mathcal{T}} \bot$.

Definition 3.7 (concept contraction). *Let $\mathcal{L}$ be a DL, S, D be two concepts in $\mathcal{L}$ and $\mathcal{T}$ be a set of axioms in $\mathcal{L}$, where both S and D are satisfiable in $\mathcal{T}$. A concept contraction problem (CCP), identified by $< \mathcal{L}, S, D, \mathcal{T} >$ is finding a pair of concepts $< G, K > \in \mathcal{L} \times \mathcal{L}$ such that $D \equiv_{\mathcal{T}} G \sqcap K$ and $K \sqcap C$ is satisfiable in $\mathcal{T}$. K is called a contraction of D according to S and $\mathcal{T}$.*

Once contraction has been applied and consistency between the supply and the demand has been regained, there is still the problem with partial specifications, i.e., it could be the case that the supply—though compatible—does not imply the demand. It is then necessary to assess what should be hypothesized in the supply in order to start the transaction with the demand. This non-standard inference is called *concept abduction* [NSDM03].

Definition 3.8 (concept abduction). *Let $\mathcal{L}$ be a DL, S, D be two concepts in $\mathcal{L}$ and $\mathcal{T}$ be a set of axioms in $\mathcal{L}$, where both S and D are satisfiable in $\mathcal{T}$. A concept abduction problem (CAP), identified by $< \mathcal{L}, S, D, \mathcal{T} >$, is finding a concept $H \in \mathcal{L}$ (hypotheses) such that $S \sqcap_{\mathcal{T}} H \sqsubseteq D$ and moreover $S \sqcap H$ is satisfiable in $\mathcal{T}$.*

Example:

Let us consider a simplified scenario in an e-marketplace. We have a demand D expressed as: "I am looking for a computer such that it must be a PC including an inkjet printer." We also have an available supply S expressed as: "Personal computer equipped with a high level laser printer." The aim is to find which parts are shared by D and S (K for keep) and which ones are not (G for give up). Formally,

$$D \equiv \mathsf{homePC} \sqcap \forall \mathsf{hasComponent.InkjetPrinter}$$

$$S \equiv \mathsf{homePC} \sqcap \forall \mathsf{hasComponent.LaserPrinter}.$$

Solving a CCP we obtain a $< G, K >$ where

$$G = \forall \mathsf{hasComponent.InkjetPrinter},$$

$$K = \mathsf{homePC}.$$

Although S and D are not identical, $K \sqcap S$ is satisfiable, hence K potentially matches S.

4

Natural Language Processing

Natural language processing (NLP) is a subfield of linguistics and artificial intelligence (AI). It studies the problems inherent to the processing and manipulation of natural language (NL). The ultimate goal of NLP is to make computers "understand" statements written in human languages. The definition of "understanding" is one of the major problems in NLP.

This chapter will cover *graphemics* (written language) only. For other topics of NLP, such as phonemics (spoken language), speech recognition, optical character recognition (OCR), machine translation, text summarization, NL generation, etc., we refer the interested reader to [All94, MS99, CEE+01, Mit04, HCG+10].

4.1 Overview and Challenges

4.1.1 Syntax, Semantics and Pragmatics

The terms syntax, semantics, and pragmatics define different things:

- *Syntax* is the study of the structure. It focuses on the form, not the meaning. For example, the sentence:

$$I \text{ movies the go to with my wife.} \tag{4.1}$$

  contains only correct words but is syntactically wrong.
- *Semantics* refers to aspects of meaning. For example, the sentence:

$$The \text{ movies went to me.} \tag{4.2}$$

  is syntactically correct but semantically wrong.
- *Pragmatics* studies the ways in which context contributes to meaning. For example, the sentence:

$$Is \text{ the window open?} \tag{4.3}$$

is syntactically and semantically correct, and may refer to a person who feels cold. This sentence can only be interpreted correctly if the reader puts it into a certain context.

Computer systems can handle syntax. The processing of the semantics of a sentence is more complex. It generally relies on the framework used to represent the semantics in a machine-readable form, e.g., a language to encode metadata (see chapter 2). Today, there is no computer system that can handle pragmatics in a reliable way.

4.1.2 Difficulties of NLP

When we as humans process language, we are continually making guesses about meaning, using our rich knowledge of the world and of the current culture to try and work out what is being communicated. For example, if asked:

$$Is\ there\ water\ in\ the\ fridge? \tag{4.4}$$

most humans would consider this question as referring to a bottle of mineral water in the fridge. In fact, we use language with a rich knowledge of "normal circumstances". When using language in these situations, we do not need to state them explicitly. They are assumed to be known to all communicators. This unspoken context may comprise 90% of a communication and allows the language which builds on this foundation to be very concise [Inm04]. This general knowledge and the reasoning abilities, are what makes humans intelligent. But computers only have very limited views of context, culture, or normal circumstances. For a computer, everything is an endless muddle of possibilities with almost no way to sort out the "normal circumstance".

NL is what we call *informal* and leaves a lot of space for *ambiguities*. For example, the question:

$$How\ was\ the\ date? \tag{4.5}$$

may refer to "a sweet, dark brown, oval fruit containing a hard stone, often eaten dried" or "a social or romantic appointment or engagement". Making computers "understand" such informalities is impossible when they analyze isolated words and even sentences.

Very often, a statistical and probabilistic approach is used to make guesses about the interpretation of ambiguities. In the above example, if most of the former NL sentences were about sports, then the question in (4.5) could be be put into that same context as well. Such data about the user's context can be collected from former interactions, e.g., quality feedback, as mentioned in chapter 5.

Another common technique in NLP is to rely on a training set or *corpus*. Large amounts of text, e.g., from newspapers, are analyzed and utilized to create statistical data about the use of words. This may allow to detect patterns in sentences that can help to interpret language accurately. Such statistical approaches to NLP are the core of *computational linguistics*.

4.1.3 Zipf's law

In 1949, George Kingsley Zipf published his theory that people generally act so as to minimize their probable average rate of work [Zip49]. Applied to linguistics, this means that while only a few words are used very often, many or most are used rarely. Computer systems can benefit from this statistical distribution among the words in a corpus.

Let us put all words from a corpus into a table which is sorted by the frequency of the words. Zipf's law states that the frequency of any word is inversely proportional to its rank in the frequency table, written:

$$f_n \approx \frac{1}{n}$$

where n is the rank of a word and f_n is the frequency of the nth word. This means that, e.g., the first word occurs approximately twice as often as the second word and the 50th word occurs approximately 3 times more often than the 150th word.

4.2 Dealing with Single Words

4.2.1 Tokenization and Tagging

A first step in NLP is **tokenization**, which denotes the action of dividing a text into its tokens. A *token* is a part of the sentence, such as a word or a number. Each token belongs to a *word category*, like nouns, verbs, and adjectives. Such categories are also called *part-of-speech* (POS) and are referenced by a *tag*, e.g., NN for noun, VV for verb, and JJ for adjective according to the *Brown* tag set [KF60] which we are using in this book. There are other tag sets, like the *British National Corpus C5* tag set and the *Penn Treebank* tag set.

In the English language, nouns, verbs and adjectives are the most important word categories. To demonstrate this, let us consider the sentence:

$$\textit{Computers are complex systems.} \qquad (4.6)$$

This sentence is composed of four tokens: "computer" and "system" are nouns, "are" (to be) is the verb, and "complex" is the adjective that describes the noun "system".

- *Nouns* (NN) refer to people, animals, concepts, and things, e.g., girl, cat, idea, and computer. Proper nouns (NNP) are names like Serge and Luxembourg.
- *Verbs* (VV) generally express the action in a sentence, e.g., I *go* to the movies and she *kicks* him hard.

- *Adjectives* (JJ) describe properties of nouns, e.g., a *red* nose and the *big* computer.

Many other word categories exist. The following incomplete list provides an overview (an exhaustive list is given in appendix C):

- *Adverbs* (RB) modify a verb in the same way that adjectives modify nouns, e.g., he moves *quickly* and she kicks him *hard.*
- *Qualifiers* (QL), e.g., very, too, extremely.
- *Prepositions* (IN), e.g., of, to, in, for, on, with, as, by, at, from.
- *Determiners* are articles (AT) (e.g., the, a, an) and demonstratives (DT) (e.g., this, that).
- *Pronouns* (PN) are substitutes for nouns, e.g., she, her, herself, mine.
- *Quantifiers* (ABN), e.g., all, many, some, any.
- *Cardinals* (CD), e.g., one, two, 123.
- *Ordinals* (OD), e.g., first, second.
- *Interrogative words* (W), e.g., who, when, how, where.
- *Conjunctions* (CC), e.g., and, or, but, if, before, although.

The action of analyzing a token and detecting its word category is commonly called **tagging**. A tool for tagging is called a *tagger*. The sentence:

$$Every\ network\ requires\ a\ protocol\ like\ TCP/IP. \qquad (4.7)$$

is tagged as follows:

token	word category	tag
Every	determiner	DT
network	noun, singular	NN
requires	verb, present tense	VVZ
a	determiner	DT
protocol	noun, singular	NN
like	preposition	IN
TCP/IP	noun, singular	NN

As mentioned above, NL is informal and may cause ambiguities. Here are some general problems while dealing with tokens:

- A token can be found in different word categories. For example, the word "blink" can be a noun (a *blink* with the eye) or a verb (*to blink* with the eye).
- Punctuation marks and special characters (like hyphens and slashes) are difficult to process, e.g., TCP/IP, error-handling, or Dot.Five can be considered as one word or as two different words. The problem is even more pronounced when dealing with abbreviations like "I fly to *Lux.* next week", where the period does not terminate the sentence. Finally, punctuation marks can be used to represent symbols and emoticons, e.g., :-).

- A sentence that contains quotation marks (e.g., a quote) may have different meanings depending on the person making the assertion.
- Whitespaces are generally used to separate words but are sometimes confusing. The most common problem is when a whitespace does not separate words, e.g., "hard disk". In some languages such as Chinese, words are never separated by blanks. The analysis of such words gets even more complicated when both parts are not adjacent, e.g., the phrasal verb "to work out". A complicated sentence could be "I can't help you with this answer, so you will have to *work* it *out* for yourself." Similar constructs are the formulations "in order to" or "because of".
- Proper names may be difficult to detect because they can contain a whitespace, e.g., "New York" or can be written in the same way as a verb or a noun, e.g., "Apple".
- Typographic conventions may vary in different countries, e.g., in French, a blank precedes an exclamation mark.
- References inside a sentence can be made, e.g., "What does the T in TCP/IP mean?"

The above list illustrates how complex the processing of complete NL sentence can get. In practice, most often heuristics are used. Generally, tools like taggers are based on the computation of probabilities and are trained over large *corpora*. For example, a tagger calculates the odds for the words "New" + whitespace + "York" being one single token (a proper name) or being two separated tokens.

Some algorithms are based on *Viterbi search* [For73]. It hinges on the observation that the most likely tag sequence from the beginning of the sentence to the current word, ending with a particular POS tag, can be computed recursively from these quantities for the previous word and the transition and emission probabilities. Such heuristic taggers have 90 - 97 % accuracy [CEE+01].

4.2.2 Morphology

Morphology is the study of the rules to form words. A given word can exist in various different morphological forms, e.g., "men" is the plural of "man" and "went" is the past simple of "to go". In terms of morphology, English is a simple language where a given word can exist in a very limited number of morphologies, i.e., four distinct forms for a regular verb and eight distinct forms for an irregular verb. There are three major types of morphological processes:

- *Inflection*: grammatical distinction by changing tense, number, and plurality, e.g., "woman" → "women" and "have" → "had".
- *Derivation*: change of syntactic category, e.g., "wide" → "widely", "soft" → "soften" and "accept" → "acceptable".

- *Compounding*: merging of two or more words into a new word, e.g., "hard" and "disk" → "hard disk".

A *morpheme* is the smallest linguistic unit that has a meaning. For example, "hard disk" is not a morpheme because it can be decomposed into "hard" and "disk". Both words cannot be further decomposed because there is no word like "ha" or "rd", therefore both are morphemes.

The inverse operation, i.e., transforming a given word into its canonical form or stem, is called *stemming*. For example, the stem of the verb "brewed" (past tense) is "brew" (infinite) and the stem of "apples" (plural) is "apple" (singular).

Lemmatization refers to a similar action with the aim of finding the *lemma* (or *lexeme*) of a word. The result of lemmatization is that possible ambiguities in the words interpretation are resolved so that a lexeme is a word with a single meaning. For example, the word "date" may have three lexemes, i.e., three dictionary entries, because it may refer to a day on a calendar, a fruit, or a romantic appointment.

To emphasize the difference between morpheme and lemma: a morpheme can have different meanings but not a lexeme. Hence, "date" is a morpheme but not a lexeme, but "date (fruit)" is a lexeme.

4.2.3 Building Words over an Alphabet

Words are built with an alphabet. An alphabet Σ is a non-empty set of symbols. The set of all possible words that can be formed through this alphabet, i.e., with these symbols, is written Σ^*. For illustration, let us consider the following alphabet Σ and the set Σ^* of all possible words that can be formed with Σ. Then we can build the language L, which is a subset of Σ^* and contains all English words ($L \subseteq \Sigma^*$):

$$\Sigma = \{a,b,c,d,e,f,g,h,i,j,k,l,m,n,o,p,q,r,s,t,u,v,w,x,y,z\}$$
$$\Sigma^* = \{a, aaaa, abad, and, are, axyz, aware,...\}$$
$$L = \{a, and, are, aware,...\}$$

4.2.4 Operations over Words

The first basic operation with an alphabet is *concatenation*, which puts two words together, written: $w_1 \bullet w_2$. For example, let $w_1 =$ "toto" and $w_2 =$ "tata", then:

$$w_1 \bullet \text{ " loves " } \bullet w_2$$

results in the string: "toto loves tata".

A second useful operation with words is the quantification of their difference. Two words are *equivalent* if they are written in the exact same way. But in some cases, due to a possible spelling error, one wants to measure the similarity of two words which are not exactly equivalent. In this case, the *edit distance* indicates how many modifications, deletions, and additions have to be made to change one word into a second word. The edit distance is also called **Levenshtein Distance** [Lev66]. The greater the Levenshtein distance, the more different the strings are. For example, the Levenshtein distance between the German word "Protokoll" and the French word "protocole" is three, because three modifications are required to turn "Protokoll" into "protocol", i.e., "P" → "p", "k" → "c", and "l" → "e".

The edit distance can be regarded in relationship with the length of the destination word to get a relative measure for the distance. In the example, the length of "protocole" is written: |protocole| = 9 and the relative edit distance between the words "Protokoll" and "protocole" is: $\frac{3}{9}$ = 33%. A question-answering system could, e.g., recognize words with a failure tolerance of 30%.

4.3 Semantic Knowledge Sources

4.3.1 Semantic relations

Two sentences can express the same meaning but use different words, e.g.:

$$I \; drive \; a \; car. \tag{4.8}$$

$$I \; drive \; an \; automobile. \tag{4.9}$$

For a computer system, this semantic equivalence between the words "car" and "automobile" is extremely difficult to detect, because pure string-comparison will not allow to find out this equivalence. Commonly, semantic resources like dictionaries or thesauri are used to analyze the semantic relation between words.

- *Hypernym* is a word with a more general meaning, e.g., "animal" is a hypernym of "cat".
- *Hyponym* is a word with a more specific meaning, e.g., "cat" is a hyponym of "animal".
- *Antonyms* are words with opposite meaning, e.g., "cold" and "hot".
- *Synonyms* are words with identical meaning, e.g., "car" and "automobile".
- *Homonyms* are words that are written the same way but have different meaning, e.g. "date" can refer to a romantic appointment, a day on a calendar, or a fruit.

By using an appropriated semantic resource, the equivalence between the words "car" and "automobile" may be made explicit; both are synonyms. Hence, a computer system may conclude that both sentences represent the same meaning.

Semantic resources that offer this kind of relations between words are typically used in expert systems to compute the semantic similarity of two

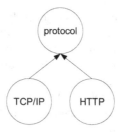

Fig. 4.1. Example of a hypernym/hyponym relation.

sentences. Also, more complicated reasoning operations are possible. For a given sentence, a more general or a more specific meaning may be computed. For example, consider the sentences:

$$The\ Internet\ uses\ TCP/IP. \tag{4.10}$$

$$Every\ network\ uses\ a\ protocol. \tag{4.11}$$

By simple string-comparison, a computer system finds out that both sentences are not the same because all the words are different. However, if the meaning of the nouns "Internet" and "network" is analyzed using a semantic resource, then a computer system can infer that "Internet" is a hyponym of "network" (see figure 4.1). Similar, "TCP/IP" is a hyponym for "protocol". Eventually, the expert system may draw the conclusion that both sentences are about the same topic (i.e., networks that use protocols) and that the first sentence is more specific than the second one.

4.3.2 Semantic resources

Machine-readable semantic resources play a key role in NLP. They allow computer-systems to read information about the meaning of tokens like relations describe above. Eventually, some kind of reasoning is possible to infer implicit knowledge from the sentence.

The building of such a semantic resource is an expensive endeavor. Therefore, most systems rely on existing resources like *WordNet* [Ma98]. Generally, such semantic resources have a tree-like structure representing the relations between words, as depicted in figure 4.1.

WordNet is an online reference system combining the design of a dictionary and a thesaurus with the rich potential of an ontological database. Instead of being arranged in alphabetical order, words are stored in a database with hierarchial properties and links.

In WordNet, every *synset* contains a group of synonymous words; different meanings of a word are in different synsets. An example of the dictionary entry for the word "protocol" is depicted in figure 4.2 showing three possible synsets for this noun:

Noun

- S: (n) **protocol**, communications protocol ((computer science) rules determining the format and transmission of data)
  - ○ *direct hyponym / full hyponym*
    - S: (n) file transfer protocol, FTP (protocol that allows users to copy files between their local system and any system they can reach on the network)
    - S: (n) hypertext transfer protocol, HTTP (a protocol (utilizing TCP) to transfer hypertext requests and information between servers and browsers)
    - S: (n) musical instrument digital interface, MIDI (a standard protocol for communication between electronic musical instruments and computers)
    - **S: (n) transmission control protocol, TCP (a protocol developed for the internet to get data from one network device to another) *TCP uses a retransmission strategy to insure that data will not be lost in transmission"***
      - ○ *direct hypernym / inherited hypernym / sister term*
      - ○ *part holonym*
    - S: (n) transmission control protocol/internet protocol, TCP/IP (a set of protocols (including TCP) developed for the internet in the 1970s to get data from one network device to another)
  - ○ *domain category*
    - S: (n) computer science, computing (the branch of engineering science that studies (with the aid of computers) computable processes and structures)
  - ○ *direct hypernym / inherited hypernym / sister term*
- S: (n) **protocol** (forms of ceremony and etiquette observed by diplomats and heads of state)
- S: (n) **protocol** (code of correct conduct) *"safety protocols," "academic protocol"*

Fig. 4.2. Dictionary entry in WordNet for "protocol".

- protocol as a communication protocol in computer science,
- forms of ceremony and etiquette observed by diplomats and heads of state,
- and code of correct conduct.

WordNet's latest version is 3.0. The database contains 155,287 words organized in 117,659 synsets. Most synsets are connected to other synsets via a number of semantic relations.

4.4 Dealing with Sentences

In this section we focus on the syntactic analysis of a complete sentence (*phrase*) instead of isolated words. As hinted at in section 4.4, a sentence is only meaningful if the words are put together in compliance with certain rules. *Syntax* is the study of the principles and rules for constructing sentences.

4.4.1 Phrase Types

A sentence (S) is generally composed of different linguistic sub-sentences. Here is a summary of these phrase types.

- *Noun phrase* (NP): a noun is usually embedded in a noun phrase. In this sub-sentence, all the details about the noun are gathered. Example of a complete noun phrase:

$$\textit{The beautiful girl from next town.} \tag{4.12}$$

- *Verb phrase* (VP): a verb is usually embedded in a verb phrase. In this sub-sentence, all the details about the verb are gathered. Example of a complete verb phrase:

$$\text{Read this book as fast as you can!} \tag{4.13}$$

- *Prepositional phrase* (PP): a prepositional phrase has a preposition as its head and generally acts as complement of and adjunct to a noun phrase and verb phrase, e.g.,

$$\text{You are like your father.} \tag{4.14}$$

where "like your father" is the prepositional phrase.
- *Adjective phrase* (AP): an adjective phrase is a phrase with a preposition or adverb as its head, e.g.,

$$\text{She is very sure of herself.} \tag{4.15}$$

where "very sure of herself" is the adjective phrase.

4.4.2 Phrase Structure

The syntactic analysis of a sentence is called *parsing*. The tool to parse a sentence is called a *parser*. The structure of a sentence can be represented as a list or tree. Let us consider the following sentence:

$$\text{Every network requires a protocol like TCP/IP.} \tag{4.16}$$

- As list:

```
(S (NP (DT Every)
       (NN network))
   (VP (VVZ requires)
       (NP (DT a)
           (NN protocol))
       (PP (IN like)
           (NN TCP/IP))))
```

- As syntax tree:

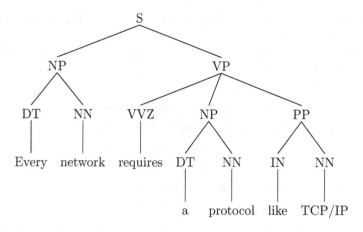

4.4.3 Grammar

A grammar is the set of rules to build words and sentences in a given language. A formal grammar in the *Chomsky hierarchy* is typically a quadruple composed of two alphabets, one with non-terminal symbols and one with terminal symbols, a set of rules, and a start symbol.

Definition 4.1 (grammar). *A grammar $G = \langle \Phi, \Sigma, R, S \rangle$ is composed of:*

- *an alphabet of non-terminal symbols Φ,*
- *an alphabet of terminal symbols Σ with $\Phi \cap \Sigma = \emptyset$,*
- *a set of rules R with each item of the form $\alpha \to \beta$, where $\alpha \in \Phi^*$ and $\beta \in (\Phi \cup \Sigma)^*$,*
- *a start symbol $S \in \Phi$.*

For purposes of illustration, let us consider the following grammar, which was used to build the above syntax tree:

G = ⟨ {S, NP, VP, DT, NN, VVZ, PP, IN, NP},
    {Every, network, requires, a, protocol, like, TCP/IP},
    {S → NP + VP,
    NP → DT + NN,
    DT → Every,
    DT → a,
    NN → network,
    NN → protocol,
    NP → TCP/IP,
    VP → VVZ + NP + PP,
    VVZ → requires,
    PP → IN + NP,
    IN → like},
    S ⟩

This kind of grammar is called *context-free*, because it can be used to form any other sentences, even if some of them make no sense. Examples of such (in)valid phrases according the above gramme are (incorrect sentences are marked with *):

$$a \ protocol \ requires \ every \ network \ like \ protocol. \tag{4.17}$$

$$a \ protocol \ requires \ a \ protocol \ like \ protocol. \tag{4.18}$$

$$* \quad a \ protocol \ like \ a \ protocol \ like \ TCP/IP. \tag{4.19}$$

$$Every \ TCP/IP \ requires \ every \ network \ like \ protocol. \tag{4.20}$$

$$* \quad The \ protocol \ requires \ a \ network. \tag{4.21}$$

$$* \quad Every \ protocol. \tag{4.22}$$

Rules in a context-free grammar must have a non-terminal symbol on the left-hand side. This restriction does not exist in a *context-sensitive* grammar where each rule is of the form:

$$S \rightarrow \emptyset$$

or

$$\alpha A \gamma \rightarrow \alpha \beta \gamma$$

with $\alpha, \beta, \gamma \in (\Phi \cup \Sigma)^*, A \in \Phi$ and $\beta \neq \emptyset$. This kind of grammar allows to form much more complex sentences. Therefore, most NLP systems are limited to context-free grammars to reduce the risk of ambiguities.

4.4.4 Formal languages

Every language is based on at least one grammar. However, different grammars can exist for the same language. Hence, new *formal languages* can be defined with grammars.

Definition 4.2 (formal language). *Let G be a grammar, then $L(G)$ is a formal language created by G and written:*

$$L(G) = \{w \in \Sigma^* \mid S \overset{*}{\Rightarrow} w\}$$

where $S \overset{*}{\Rightarrow} w$ stands for all (direct) combinations and derivations of words that are possible by starting from S and ending as terminal symbol.

4.4.5 Phrase structure ambiguities

The problem of parsing a sentence is that a large number of different interpretations are possible and result in *syntactic ambiguities*. A famous example is the sentence:

$$The \ horse \ raced \ past \ the \ barn \ fell. \tag{4.23}$$

This is a so called *garden path sentence* because the reader thinks that the sentence must be finished after the word "barn" [Bev70]. The sentence can be parsed as follows:

- First syntax tree:

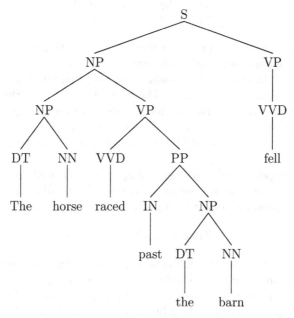

- Second syntax tree:

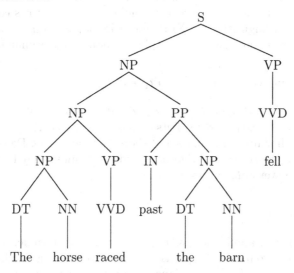

A computer can never determine in a reliable way which interpretation is the best. Generally, a probabilistic approach is used to rank different parses and to give preference to the most "likely" one. Such systems are called *probabilistic context-free grammars* (PCFG).

For purposes of illustration, let us consider the following extract of a PCFG that has been used to build both syntax trees:

$$\begin{array}{lll} \text{S} & \rightarrow \text{NP} + \text{VP} & 1.00 \\ \text{NP} & \rightarrow \text{NP} + \text{VP} & 0.63 \\ \text{NP} & \rightarrow \text{NP} + \text{PP} & 0.37 \end{array}$$

There are two rules to process a noun phrase (NP). Both are possible and create the ambiguity depicted in the above syntax trees.

In the far right column, a probability is indicated which is either set by a human or based on empirical data. The example shows that the odds for NP-rule 1 are higher than for rule 2. Hence, in case of an ambiguity, the system may give preference to rule 1 rather than to rule 2. In our example, this means that the first syntax tree would be considered more accurate than the second one.

Such strategies to solve phrase ambiguities work well with small sets of phrases and with a limited domain or context. They fail if the parser were to deal with texts covering different domains. A classical example is the sentence:

$$\textit{Time flies like an arrow.} \tag{4.24}$$

This sentence can be interpreted differently depending the context it is read. For example, are there beings called "time flies" which like arrows or does time have the speed of an arrow? A third possibility: time flies like an arrow (in a straight path) and not like a bird (generally unpredictable up-and-down movement). As a parser only checks syntax rules (and not the sense of a sentence), a multitude of different syntactically correct trees could be built. Thus, computer linguistics and NLP aim to develop grammars that cover most of NL. Such grammars get very complex without getting unambiguous.

4.4.6 Alternative parsing techniques

The technique of *full syntactic parsing* described above applies a formal grammar and analyzes the phrase in all its details. As stated earlier, such techniques work well with simple grammars and short sentences only. Depending on the application, a less severe and rigorous parsing technique may be sufficient and might cause fewer ambiguities.

Shallow Parsing

For some types of application, *shallow parsing* may be sufficient. The aim of this technique is to partition a phrase into non-overlapping chunks. Each *chunk* has one or more words and is assigned to a category, e.g., noun or preposition. The head-word of each chunk is marked. For example, the following sentence might be chunked as:

$$\textit{Every network requires a protocol.} \tag{4.25}$$

$$[_N \; Every \; network^H][_V \; requires^H][_N \; a \; protocol^H]$$

This sentence is partitioned into three chunks. The first chunk represents the noun "every network", where "network" is the head of the noun. The second chunk is a single verb "requires". The third chunk represents the noun "a protocol" with "protocol" as head of the chunk.

Partial Parsing

It is sufficient for some kinds of applications to detect patterns in a phrase. This technique is known as *partial parsing*. A pattern could be: noun phrases (NP) + verb phrases (VP). In that case, only this kind of phrases would be identified without being parsed any further. More sophisticated approaches assign grammatical functions to noun phrases (subject, direct object, indirect object) and give partial information on attachments. Algorithms for partial parsing often rely on the output of a tagger.

One striking advantage of this technique is that the resulting syntax tree becomes rather flat and easier to process. Furthermore, fewer ambiguities will be encountered while parsing.

For the above pattern and the sentence in (4.25), the syntax tree resulting from a partial parse would be:

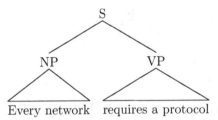

A simple way to approximate such a parser would be to remove rules from a general grammar. The grammar required to parse the above tree would be reduced to: S → NP + VP.

Other Parsing Techniques

Other parsing techniques are *dependency parsing, context-free parsing* and *unification-based parsing*.

4.5 Multi-Language

Different languages have different grammars. This makes the development of multi-language systems even more complicated, especially if the language has to be detected automatically. Generally, a parser or tagger is built for one language only. To stretch out the differences between languages, let us have a look at an example of a simple sentence and depict the resulting syntax trees for English, German, and French.

English: *Every network requires a protocol.*   (4.26)

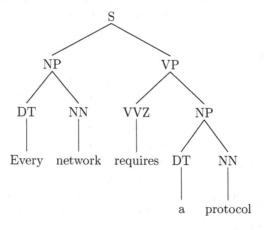

German: *Jedes Netzwerk benötigt ein Protokoll.*   (4.27)

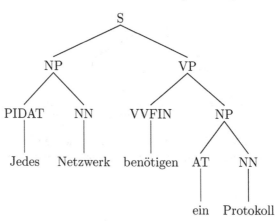

Here, PIDAT stands for attributive indefinite pronoun with determiner (German: attributierendes Indefinitpronomen mit Determiner), VVFIN stands for finite verb form (German: finite Verbform), and AT stands for article (German: Artikel).

French: *Chaque réseau a besoin d'un protocole.*   (4.28)

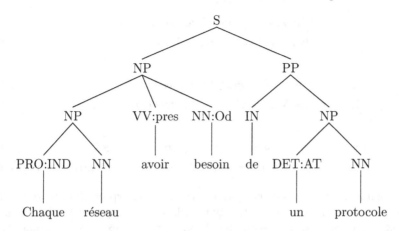

Here PRO:IND stands for indefinite pronoun (French: pronon indéfini), VV:pres stands for verb in present simple tense (French: verbe à l'indicatif présent), IN stands for preposition (French: préposition), and DET:AT stands for determiner / article (French: déterminant / article).

4.6 Semantic Interpretation

The ultimate goal of NLP is the automatic interpretation of NL, i.e., the translation of NL into a machine-readable formalism with clear semantics. Commonly, NL is transformed into formulas of some logics, e.g., first order logic (FOL) or Description Logics (DL). More generally, the representation of context-independent meaning is called the *logical form*. The process of mapping a sentence to its logical form is called *semantic interpretation*.

There are many rules about how to interpret tokens and complete sentences. As stated above, the more accurate a NL sentence should be translated into a logical form, the more complex the required grammar gets. For the sake of illustration, let us fix the following rules and consider only simple sentences:

- Nouns are translated into unary predicates.
- Verbs are translated into binary predicates.
- Auxiliary verbs are ignored.
- Proper names are translated into objects.
- For all variables, the universal quantifier ($\forall$) is used unless the formulation "there is a" is found in the sentence.
- All other parts-of-speech are ignored.

Here are examples of semantic interpretations according the above set of rules:

$$\text{NL:} \quad \textit{TCP/IP is a protocol.} \qquad (4.29)$$

$$\text{FOL:} \quad \textit{Protocol}(TCP/IP) \qquad (4.30)$$

NL: *There is a protocol named TCP/IP.*   (4.31)

FOL: $(\exists x)Protocol(x) \wedge hasName(x,'TCP/IP')$ (4.32)

NL: *Every network requires a protocol.*   (4.33)

FOL: $(\forall x)(\forall y)Network(x) \rightarrow (Protocol(y) \rightarrow require(x,y))$ (4.34)

NL: *There is a network that requires a protocol.*   (4.35)

FOL: $(\exists x)(\forall y)Network(x) \wedge (Protocol(y) \rightarrow require(x,y))$ (4.36)

Depending on the expected granularity of the interpretation, more precise rules have to be elaborated to strictly translate an NL sentence into its logical formulae. Hence, with increasing precision, the complexity of the translation grows and results in more ambiguities. Some of these problems have already been mentioned in section 4.2.1.

Here is an example of a sentence which is relatively easy to understand by humans, but extremely complicated for a machine to interpret:

Serge says that he knows that all the networks he knows use TCP/IP.
(4.37)

In practise, the expected precision of the interpretation most often depends on the application. All systems which interact with people have some knowledge about their users' expectations and their domain of application. A common method is stereotyping; grouping of people into so-called *folksonomies*, which are groups (or classes) of people with common properties. If the application is about understanding the sense of a query entered in NL, then a more greedy algorithm may be used. If, however, an exact translation is expected, then the interpretation of quantifiers, negations, passive voice, etc. have to be processed.

To further illustrate the difficulties of interpreting NL, let us consider the following sentence:

Most networks use TCP/IP.   (4.38)

This example of using a quantifier can only be translated into a logic of higher order, i.e.,

$$\lambda x[(\exists y)Network(y) \wedge use(y,x)](TCP/IP).$$

Here, quantified NPs are interpreted as generalized quantifiers which correspond to sets of sets (or properties of properties). "Most networks" denotes the set of sets that contain networks using TCP/IP. A quantificational determiner like "most" is mapped to a λ-term.

In fact, determining the scope of quantifiers and operators in the logical form is a very complex problem that not only involves using lexical, syntactic, and semantic information, but is also strongly influenced by context. For example:

Everyone thinks that TCP and UDP are connection-less protocols.   (4.39)

It is not evident for a machine to identify if "everyone" refers to "TCP", "UDP", or both. The real challenge of NLP therefore lies in the attempt to make computers emulate the cognitive processes of the human brain.

5

Information Retrieval

The representation of information in electronic form, its storage in database systems and the retrieval of information from such databases are one of the most important fields in computer-science. Knowledge representation, intelligent content management, and multimedia information retrieval are modern expressions of current research fields. However, basics from "classical" information retrieval (IR) like indexing, retrieval models, and retrieval evaluation are still valid and remain important concepts.

IR has gained in importance because it is no longer limited to the study of finding material in databases. Modern IR is also about intelligent user interfaces, user feedback, and tagging to name but a few. The term database itself has been extended to new areas like digital libraries and the World Wide Web (WWW). Also, databases are no longer collections of (un)structured textual documents but contain more complex content, like audio and video documents.

5.1 Retrieval Process

Generally, a database system is dynamic: both content and query change in time. In some systems, the content may be more stable and the queries may vary, e.g., an online archive where the content is rarely updated. In other systems, the content may change frequently but the queries remain unchanged, e.g., a stock marked.

The retrieval of documents from a storage can be depicted as a process of several steps (see figure 5.1). On the user-side, an information need is specified and formalized in a query, e.g., in SQL. On the system-side, the documents in the database are indexed to improve the search performance (see section 5.2). In a matching process, candidate documents are retrieved and eventually ranked according their relevance. Possible user feedback may further improve the retrieval results.

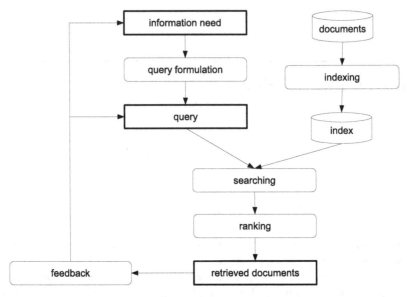

Fig. 5.1. Schema of the retrieval process.

5.2 Document Indexation and Weighting

5.2.1 Index of terms

Most retrieval models use an *index of terms*. Instead of the system browsing through complete documents, only the index of terms is used to decide whether a document is relevant or not. This increases the performance of the complete retrieval process.

The terms in the index are well chosen words and stand for the context of all documents in the collection. The index of terms can be created manually by an expert who has enough knowledge about the documents in the collection. It can also be created (semi-)automatically through the identification and extraction of index terms from the content and the metadata of the documents.

The size of an index can be approximated by *Heaps' law* [Hea78] that says:

$$V = \lambda \cdot n^\beta$$

where V is the number of index terms and n is the number of words in the collection. λ and β are free parameters determined empirically, e.g., $30 \leq \lambda \leq 100$ and $\beta \approx 0,5$. Obviously, Heaps' law only fits for large document collections.

The size of the index grows with the quantity and the size of the documents in the collection. There are different optimization techniques to reduce the size of an index in order to keep only the most relevant and representative terms, e.g.,

- ignore case sensitivity,
- use the canonical form of words (e.g., verbs in the infinitive form and nouns in the singular),
- ignore punctuation marks,
- remove semantically irrelevant words, e.g., articles.

Some of the above techniques are based on natural language (NL) operations like *tokenization* and *stemming* (see chapter 4).

A complementary and more advanced technique is to use a *dictionary of terms* (or thesaurus) with synonymy-relations. The advantage of this technique is that the same index term can stand for different words. For example, the term "car" is stored in the index. When the word "automobile" is encountered in a document or query, then the database system can refer to a thesaurus, find out that this word is semantically equivalent to the index term "car" and process it as such.

Definition 5.1 (index of terms). *The set of documents in the collection is written $D = \{d_1, ..., d_N\}$ and $K = \{k_1, ..., k_n\}$ is the set of all index terms, with $N \in \mathbb{N}_+$ the number of documents and $n \in \mathbb{N}_+$ the number of index terms.*

Example

Let us consider the following text for indexation:

All networks need at least one protocol. Protocols have different tasks like flow-control and error-checking. TCP/IP is a protocol widely used in the Internet and in other networks.

Let us decide to consider only nouns and verbs to build the index of terms. All other words, including auxiliary verbs are ignored.

All ⟨networks⟩ ⟨need⟩ at least one ⟨protocol⟩. ⟨Protocols⟩ have different ⟨tasks⟩ like ⟨flow-control⟩ and ⟨error-checking⟩. ⟨TCP/IP⟩ is a ⟨protocol⟩ widely ⟨used⟩ in the ⟨Internet⟩ and in other ⟨networks⟩.

In a next step, we transform all index terms into their canonical form and into lowercase, e.g., *networks → network, TCP/IP → tcp/ip*, and *used → use*. Finally, the following index of terms can be set up:

$K = \{$ network, need, protocol, task, flow-control, error-checking,

tcp/ip, use, internet$\}$

5.2.2 Weighting

A *weight* that represents the term's relevancy is associated to each index term. The simplest approach is to use binary weights, which means that an index term is either present or absent. The weight could be the number of occurrences of a term, i.e., the *term frequency (tf)*.

The weighting of terms can be improved by considering the context of the documents in the collection. For example, if a database is about sports, then a word like "sport" will occur very often and probably in all the documents. Hence, it is less relevant to distinguish the similarity between documents. Therefore, a common technique is to compute the *inverse document frequency (idf)*, which takes into account the frequency of a term over a set of documents (instead of one document only) and assigns less importance to words that appear very often. The idf_i for an index term k_i is given by:

$$idf_i = log\frac{N}{n_i} \tag{5.1}$$

where N is the total number of documents and n_i the number of documents in which the index term k_i appears. Finally, a more optimal weight is:

$$w_{i,j} = tf_{i,j} \cdot idf_i \tag{5.2}$$

which assigns to each term k_i in a document d_j a weight $w_{i,j}$ that is:

- highest when k_i occurs many times within a small number of documents,
- lower when k_i occurs fewer times in a document or occurs in many documents,
- lowest when k_i occurs very often in virtually every document.

Definition 5.2 (weight of terms and index vector). *Let $D = \{d_1, ..., d_N\}$ be the set of documents in the collection and $K = \{k_1, ..., k_n\}$ the set of all index terms. A weight $w_{i,j}$ with $i \in [1..n]$ and $j \in [1..N]$ is associated with each index term k_i of a document d_j. An index term vector $\vec{d} = \{w_{1,j}, ..., w_{n,j}\}$ is then associated to each document d_j.*

Example

Let us suppose that we have the documents d_1, d_2, d_3 and d_4 ($N = 4$) in a database and an index of three terms ($n = 3$) with the following term frequencies:

	tf_1	tf_2	tf_3
d_1	0	2	1
d_2	0	3	4
d_3	0	2	0
d_4	1	0	0
n_i	1	3	2

This table expresses that document d_1 contains zero occurrences of index term k_1, two occurrences of index term k_2 and one occurrences of index term k_3. The following table depicts the inverse document frequency as defined in (5.1) and the weight as defined in (5.2):

	idf_1	w_1	idf_2	w_2	idf_3	w_3
d_1	0,60	0,00	0,12	0,25	0,30	0,30
d_2	0,60	0,00	0,12	0,37	0,30	1,20
d_3	0,60	0,00	0,12	0,25	0,30	0,00
d_4	0,60	0,60	0,12	0,00	0,30	0,00

In terms of vectors, the four documents are represented with their respective weights as follows:

$$\vec{d_1} = \begin{pmatrix} 0,00 \\ 0,25 \\ 0,30 \end{pmatrix} \quad \vec{d_2} = \begin{pmatrix} 0,00 \\ 0,37 \\ 1,20 \end{pmatrix} \quad \vec{d_3} = \begin{pmatrix} 0,00 \\ 0,25 \\ 0,00 \end{pmatrix} \quad \vec{d_4} = \begin{pmatrix} 0,60 \\ 0,00 \\ 0,00 \end{pmatrix} \quad (5.3)$$

or as Boolean vectors:

$$\vec{d_1} = \begin{pmatrix} 0 \\ 1 \\ 1 \end{pmatrix} \quad \vec{d_2} = \begin{pmatrix} 0 \\ 1 \\ 1 \end{pmatrix} \quad \vec{d_3} = \begin{pmatrix} 0 \\ 1 \\ 0 \end{pmatrix} \quad \vec{d_4} = \begin{pmatrix} 1 \\ 0 \\ 0 \end{pmatrix} \quad (5.4)$$

Weighting a HTML document

The structure of an XML document and the elements used can be considered in the weighting of index terms because they are semantic information about the relevancy of the content. We will limit our explanation to an example of a HTML document (see [MRS08] for more details).

```
<body>
  <h1>Sportsmen and kicks</h1>
  <h2>The sportsmen</h2>
  Here are some famous sports sportsmen:
  <ul>
    <li>Serge Linckels has been practising Taekwondo
        since 1987.</li>
    <li>David Arendt has been practising since 1991.</li>
  </ul>

  <h2>The kicks</h2>
  There are different kicks like the side kick,
  called 'yop chagi' and the round-house kick,
  called 'dollyo chagi'.
</body>
```

Let us set the rule that each word is indexed, i.e., the value of each text-node. Further, the weight of each index term is computed according to its frequency and by considering a supplementary *score* ℓ associated to the HTML-tag in which it is nested. For this purpose, let us set the following rules:

- a term k_i in an `<h1>`-tag has a score $\ell_i = 3$,
- a term k_i in an `<h2>`-tag has a score $\ell_i = 2$, and
- a term k_i in the `<body>`-tag has a score $\ell_i = 1$.

The integer assigned to each score is of minor importance as long as it is fair, i.e., being the same for each document. In our example, the weight $w_{i,j}$ for each index term k_i in the document d_j is computed as follows:

$$w_{i,j} = \sum_{i=1}^{n} tf_i \cdot \ell_i$$

where f_i is the term frequency of the index term k_i and ℓ_i is the supplementary score relative to HTML-tag in which the term is nested.

If we consider the following index terms $K = \{\text{sportsman, kick}\}$ and suppose that the values of the text-nodes are transformed into their canonical form and into lowercase, then the weights for the index terms are the following:

i	k_i	tf_i		w_i
1	sportsman	$1 \times$ `<h1>`	$1 \cdot 3 = 3$	
		$1 \times$ `<h2>`	$1 \cdot 2 = 2$	
		$1 \times$ `<body>`	$1 \cdot 1 = 1$	
			total:	$3 + 2 + 1 = 6$
2	kick	$1 \times$ `<h2>`	$1 \cdot 2 = 2$	
		$3 \times$ `<body>`	$3 \cdot 1 = 3$	
			total:	$2 + 3 = 5$

The table shows that the index-term k_2 "kick" is found once in an `<h2>`-tag and three times in the `<body>`-body tag. As the score for an `<h2>`-tag is 2 and for the `<body>`-tag is 1, then the total weight is: $w_2 = 1 \cdot 2 + 3 \cdot 1 = 5$.

The approach above illustrated can be improved by considering the hierarchy of the elements. The tree-structure of the above HTML-document is depicted in figure 5.2. A possibility could be to assign a higher score to text-nodes in branches with shorter pathes than those in deeper branches.

5.3 Retrieval Models

In IR, documents are retrieved if they match a given user *query*. Similar to the index of terms, a query is a vector of index terms written: $\vec{q} = \{k_1, ..., k_n\}$.

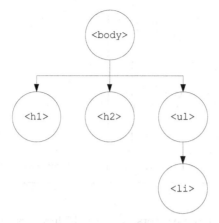

Fig. 5.2. Representation of the structure of a HTML document as tree.

Different retrieval models exist for the computation of the *similarity* between the query and each of the documents in the database, e.g., the Boolean model, the vector model, and the probabilistic model (see [BYRN99, MRS08] for further reading).

In general, given a user query q and a set of documents D, the similarity-function is written:

$$sim(q, d \mid d \in D).$$

The similarity quantifies the relevancy of a document from the collection to the query. The yielded documents can eventually be ranked according their relevancy.

5.3.1 Boolean Model

Most search engines use the Boolean retrieval model. The algorithm is simple and easy to implement. queries are specified as Boolean expressions making an index term either absent or present ($w_{i,j} \in [0,1]$) and a document either relevant or not relevant to a query.

Example

The user makes the following query:

$$q = k_1 \wedge (k_2 \vee \neg k_3).$$

The truth table 5.1 shows that the above Boolean query can be transformed into the following disjunction of conjunctive vectors:

$$\vec{q} = \begin{pmatrix} 1 \\ 0 \\ 0 \end{pmatrix} \vee \begin{pmatrix} 1 \\ 1 \\ 0 \end{pmatrix} \vee \begin{pmatrix} 1 \\ 1 \\ 1 \end{pmatrix}.$$

k_1	k_2	k_3	$k_1 \vee \neg k_2$	$k_1 \wedge (k_2 \vee \neg k_3)$
0	0	0	1	0
0	0	1	0	0
0	1	0	1	0
0	1	1	1	0
1	0	0	1	1
1	0	1	0	0
1	1	0	1	1
1	1	1	1	1

Table 5.1. Truth table for the Boolean query.

Compared to the index-vectors in (5.4) which represent the documents in the database, only document d_4 is a match. Partial matches like document d_3 are not possible in the Boolean model.

Definition 5.3 (similarity in the Boolean model). *The similarity of a document d to the query q is defined as:*

$$sim(q, d_j) = \begin{cases} 1 & \text{if } \exists \vec{q_c} \in \vec{q} \mid \vec{q_c} = \vec{d_j} \\ 0 & \text{otherwise} \end{cases}$$

where $\vec{q_c}$ is a component of the disjunctive vector $\vec{q}$.

There are a lot of improvements of the classical Boolean model. We summarize two of them:

- Considering the term frequency (tf).
  A higher score is assigned to documents where query-terms appear more frequently. The candidate-documents can then be ranked by this supplementary score.
- Considering the order of terms.
  Words can appear in the document in a different order than they appear in the query. This raises the problem that the following two documents would have equal scores: d_1="Serge performs a kick and no punch" and d_2="Serge performs a punch and no kick".

5.3.2 Vector Model

The vector model assigns non-binary weights to each index term, making it possible to rank documents by their degree of similarity. The relevancy of a document d_j to a query q, i.e., the similarity of the vector $\vec{d_j}$ to the vector $\vec{q}$, is generally computed by the cosine of the angle between both vectors:

$$sim(q, d_j) = cos \, \Theta.$$

For example, if we have the query $\vec{q}$, the documents $\vec{d_1}$ and $\vec{d_2}$, as well as:

$$cos(\vec{q}, \vec{d_1}) > cos(\vec{q}, \vec{d_2}) \quad \Leftrightarrow \quad |\vec{q} - \vec{d_1}| < |\vec{q} - \vec{d_2}|$$

then this implies that d_1 is closer to q, i.e., more relevant to the query. We suppose that these vectors are normalized; if this were not the case, longer vectors, i.e., vectors that represent longer documents, would have an unfair advantage and get ranked higher than shorter ones.

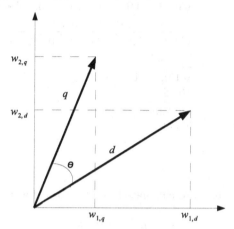

Fig. 5.3. The similarity of the vectors $\vec{q}$ and $\vec{d}$.

Definition 5.4 (similarity in the vector model). *The similarity of a document d to the query q is defined as:*

$$sim(q, d_j) = \frac{\vec{q} \cdot \vec{d}}{|\vec{q}| \cdot |\vec{d}|}$$

where the numerator represents the dot product (or inner product) of the vectors $\vec{q}$ and $\vec{d}$, and the denominator is the product of the Euclidean lengths of both vectors, resulting in:

$$sim(q, d_j) = \frac{\sum_{i=1}^{n} w_{i,q} \cdot w_{i,j}}{\sqrt{\sum_{i=1}^{n} w_{i,q}^2} \cdot \sqrt{\sum_{i=1}^{n} w_{i,j}^2}}$$

Example

Let us suppose that the user makes the query represented by the vector:

$$\vec{q} = \begin{pmatrix} 0,5 \\ 0,9 \\ 0 \end{pmatrix}$$

emphasizing the index term k_2 over index k_1. The similarity of the query q to the documents d_1 to d_4 and their respective vectors as shown in (5.3), can then be computed. The detail of the calculus for d_1 is shown below.

$$
\begin{aligned}
sim(q, d_1) &= \frac{\sum_{i=1}^{n} w_{i,q} \cdot w_{i,j}}{\sqrt{\sum_{i=1}^{n} w_{i,q}^2} \cdot \sqrt{\sum_{i=1}^{n} w_{i,j}^2}} \\
&= \frac{0.5 \cdot 0 + 0.9 \cdot 0.25 + 0 \cdot 0.3}{\sqrt{0.5^2 + 0.9^2 + 0^2} \cdot \sqrt{0^2 + 0.25^2 + 0.3^2}} \\
&= \frac{0 + 0.225 + 0}{\sqrt{0.25 + 0.81 + 0} \cdot \sqrt{0 + 0.0625 + 0.09}} \\
&= \frac{0.225}{\sqrt{1.06} \cdot \sqrt{01525}} \\
&= \frac{0.225}{0.40206} \\
sim(q, d_1) &= 0.5596
\end{aligned}
$$

The following results are calculated in an identical way:

$$ sim(q, d_2) = 0,2576 $$

$$ sim(q, d_3) = 0,8742 $$

$$ sim(q, d_4) = 0,4856 $$

By sorting the documents by their similarity we get the following ranking: best match is by far d_3, then d_1, followed by d_4, and finally d_2.

5.3.3 Probabilistic Model

In the probabilistic model, an IR system computes the "likelihood" that a subset of documents is relevant to a user query. An index term can either be absent or present in a document; weights are all binary. This means that the frequency in which an index term occurs inside a document is not considered.

The database is divided into two subsets: the relevant documents denoted R and the non-relevant documents denoted $\overline{R}$. Initial guesses about these subsets are made to start the retrieval process. After each retrieval, the probabilities are recalculated (with or without human intervention) so that the next retrieval is likely to be more accurate.

Example

To illustrate the principle of the probabilistic model, let us consider a database
with 10.000 documents and a query that contains only the index term k
(see figure 5.4). Suppose that 1.000 documents contain the index term k.
Experts have found out that only 11 documents from the complete database
are relevant to the query, of which 1 contains the index term k.

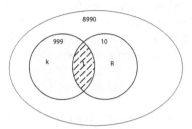

Fig. 5.4. Collection of documents and a query term k.

The interesting observation is that the chance of getting a relevant document is greater by picking a document randomly from the non-indexed set
of documents $(1 : 1.000 = 0.0010)$ than by picking it from the index set
$(10 : 9.000 = 0.0011)$. This means that if a document contains the index term
k, it has a probability of $1/11$ to be relevant. In other words, not all documents
with the index term must be relevant. During the retrieval of documents, i.e.,
after a subset of documents have been analyzed, this probability is updated,
e.g., by asking the user for feedback. If the next document containing the
keyword is retrieved and confirmed as relevant, then the probability will be
change to $2/12$.

The probabilistic model works best over large documents and long queries,
e.g., queries with a lot of keywords. Generally, search engines on the WWW
deal with very little input from the user, e.g., one or two keywords. Therefore,
the probabilistic model is less adapted for Web search engines.

This model is widely used in spam filters, where the quality of the filtering
needs to be improved in time. For example, incoming e-mail is analyzed and
marked either as spam or not spam according to some criterion. If the e-mail
is marked as not spam and remains in the inbox folder, but the user moves
it to the junk-mail folder, then the spam filter will "learn" from its wrong
decision and may yield better results next time.

Definition 5.5 (similarity in the probabilistic model). *The similarity
of a document d_j to the query q is defined as:*

$$sim(q, d_j) \approx \sum_{i=1}^{n} log \frac{P(k_i|R)}{1 - P(k_i|R)} + log \frac{1 - P(k_i|\overline{R})}{P(k_i|\overline{R})}$$

where R is the set of the relevant documents, $\overline{R}$ the set of non-relevant documents, $P(k_i|R)$ stands for the probability that the index term k_i is present in a document randomly selected from the set R and $P(k_i|\overline{R})$ stands for the probability that the index term k_i is present in a document randomly selected from the set $\overline{R}$.

The above definition is explained in detail in appendix E.

Relevance feedback of the user is often used in the probabilistic model. After a first set of candidate documents from the estimated subset R is retrieved, some interaction with the user is required to validate these results. Based on the relevance judgements of the user, the initial guesses are adapted. This step can be repeated until the user is satisfied.

5.3.4 Page Rank

The PageRank algorithm is commonly associated with *Google search*, although it is the University of Standford that holds the patent and grants exclusive usage rights to Google Inc. The original algorithm was invented by Larray Page, co-founder of Google Inc.

The ingenious principle of PageRank is that it does not depend on the query; it is a so-called static ranking function [BP98]. The hyperlink structure of the WWW is used to determine the quality of a Web page, i.e., the PageRank. If a hyperlink from a "trusted Web page" points to a page, then this referenced page is of higher importance.

The similarity of a Web page to a query can rely on PageRank by using a classical model, e.g., Boolean model, to identify a set of relevant Web pages. These pages can then be sorted according their PageRank.

The PageRank of a Web page is defined recursively and depends on the number and PageRank of all Web pages that link to it. Such links are commonly called *incoming links*.

The algorithm has evolved since its introduction in 1998 and there exist different variations, especially about the value of a *smoothing factor* λ. The smoothing factor was introduced due to the problem with zero probabilities. Some Web pages might have no incoming links, which would result in a zero PageRank. Other Web pages might have no outgoing links. This smoothing factor is uniformly distributed over all pages and solves this problem.

Definition 5.6 (PageRank). *The similarity of a document d to the query q is influence by the PageRank of the document. PageRank relies on the link structure as an indicator of an individual Web page's value and is written:*

$$PR(p_i) = \frac{1-\lambda}{N} + \lambda \cdot \sum_{j|p_j \text{ links to } p_i} \frac{PR(p_j)}{L(p_j)}$$

where N is the number of documents, $L(p_j)$ the function that returns the number of outgoing links of the Web page p_j and λ a smoothing factor.

Example

For the sake of simplicity, let us consider a Web of only four ($N = 4$) pages: A, B, C, and D (see figure 5.5).

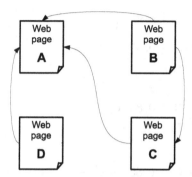

Fig. 5.5. Example of a hyperlink structure.

The following table shows the number of incoming- and outgoing links for each Web page:

	incoming	outgoing
A	3	0
B	0	2
C	1	1
D	0	1

PageRank is based on a first assumption that the probability that the user clicks on a Web page is equally distributed among all pages. In the above example, the initial PageRank for each Web page is: $PR(A) = 0.25$, $PR(B) = 0.25$, $PR(C) = 0.25$, and $PR(D) = 0.25$.

As the structure of the Web changes frequently, the PageRank has to be recalculated. This is done when Google updates its index database. A Web page's PageRank is then recursively calculated by considering the PageRank of the Web pages that link to it. By assuming a smoothing factor $\lambda = 0,85$, the PageRank for each Web page becomes:

$$PR(p_i) = \frac{1 - \lambda}{N} + \lambda \cdot \sum_{j|p_j \text{links to } p_i} \frac{PR(p_j)}{L(p_j)}$$

$$PR(p_i) = \frac{1 - 0,85}{4} + 0,85 \cdot \sum_{j|p_j \text{links to } p_i} \frac{PR(p_j)}{L(p_j)}$$

$$PR(p_i) = 0,0375 + 0,85 \cdot \sum_{j|p_j \text{links to } p_i} \frac{PR(p_j)}{L(p_j)}$$

Which would result in the following individual PageRanks:

$$PR(A) = 0,0375 + 0,85 \cdot \left(\frac{PR(B)}{L(B)} + \frac{PR(C)}{L(C)} + \frac{PR(D)}{L(D)} \right)$$

$$PR(A) = 0,0375 + 0,85 \cdot \left(\frac{0,25}{2} + \frac{0,25}{1} + \frac{0,25}{1} \right)$$

$$PR(A) = 0,0375 + 0,85 \cdot 0,625$$

$$PR(A) = 0,56875$$

$$PR(B) = 0,0375 + 0,85 \cdot 0$$

$$PR(B) = 0,0375$$

$$PR(C) = 0,0375 + 0,85 \cdot \frac{PR(B)}{L(B)}$$

$$PR(C) = 0,0375 + 0,85 \cdot \frac{0,25}{2}$$

$$PR(C) = 0,0375 + 0,85 \cdot 0,125$$

$$PR(C) = 0,14375$$

$$PR(D) = 0,0375 + 0,85 \cdot 0$$

$$PR(D) = 0,0375$$

This process can be repeated until the values do not change anymore. The following table provides an overview of the next iterations:

	initial	1	2	3	4
PR(A)	0,25	0,56875	0,20750	0,13073	0,13073
PR(B)	0,25	0,03750	0,03750	0,03750	0,03750
PR(C)	0,25	0,14375	0,05344	0,05344	0,05344
PR(D)	0,25	0,03750	0,03750	0,03750	0,03750

The above table shows that the PageRank will not change anymore after iteration 3. Finally, if Web pages B and C were yielded as candidate documents, then Web page C would be given preference over B because it has a higher PageRank.

5.3.5 Semantic Distance

A new model of computing similarities is based on the notion of *semantic distance*. The particularity of this model is not to compute the similarity between a query and a document, but to quantify their difference. If the difference is small, then the document is assumed to be closer to the query and therefore more relevant.

In the former models, the query and the documents were represented as conjunctions of index terms. This model was designed to work on a more abstract level by considering semantic descriptions, which are expressed in a knowledge representation formalisms like the Resource Description Framework (RDF), the Web Ontology Language (OWL), or Description Logics (DL). These formalisms are described in chapters 2 and 3.

This model does not rely on index terms, but is based on computing the *semantic difference* between a query and a document by using certain reasoning services. Therefore, the documents identified as relevant are the result of logical inference rather than statistical or probabilistic evaluation of index terms.

There are several algorithms to compute the semantic distances, like k *nearest neighbor*. An overview of various algorithms is provided in [SBPK06]. We summarize below the following algorithms for computing the semantic distance: pattern matching, concept abduction, concept covering problem, and best concept cover.

Pattern Matching

The algorithm for matching documents transforms a query into a pattern and identifies matches among the documents in the collection, an exact match or a more specific one [Küs01]. This algorithm is explained in detail in section 3.4.2. Although this is an excellent solution for comparing complete documents, it is less appropriate for IR systems that work with short queries.

Concept Abduction

The concept abduction problem (CAP) was initially designed to find an optimal equilibrium between a demand and a supply [CNS+03]. This algorithm is explained in detail in section 3.4.2. The algorithm was implemented in a project for semantic-based discovery of matches and negotiation spaces in an e-marketplace. It is stated as follows: compute the hypotheses that a supply is relevant to a given demand. One of the weaknesses of this solution is that it does not always return an optimal answer.

Concept Cover

The concept covering problem is about creating a conjunction of documents, i.e., the covers, which has all information required by a given query [HLRT02, BHyP+06]. This algorithm is explained in detail in section 3.4.2. It relies on the computation of minimal transversals in a hypergraph [KS05]. Similar approaches were explored in the field of artificial intelligence in the 1980s as so-called "Truth Maintenance Systems" (TMS).

Best Concept Cover

This algorithm is a modification of the concept covering problem as explained above. However, instead of returning a conjunction of documents, it aims to find few and short answers, i.e., single documents, which deliver the best possible answer, even if it is not a perfect answer. This solution will be explained in detail in section 8.

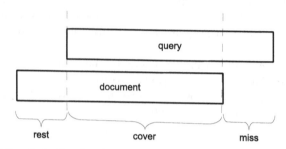

Fig. 5.6. Graphical illustration of the *Miss* and *Rest*.

To illustrate the principle of this algorithm, consider the query $q = k_2 \wedge k_5$ and the document $d = k_1 \wedge k_2 \wedge k_3$ (see figure 5.6). A *cover* is defined as the information that the query and the document have in common, here: $cover = k_2$. The missing part, i.e., the data that is required by the query but not delivered by the document is: $miss = k_5$. The data that the document delivers additionally but which was not required by the query is: $rest = k_3$.

The semantic distance between the query and a document is computed by quantifying the miss and rest. The smaller both are, the closer the document is to the query.

5.3.6 Other Models

A multitude of extensions and alternative retrieval models exist. The following list is not exhaustive and provides a reference for the interested reader:

- Extended Boolean model (combination of Boolean- and vector space model)
- Generalized vector space model
- Latent semantic indexing model
- Fuzzy set model
- Neural network model
- Bayesian network
- Belief network model

5.4 Retrieval Evaluation

An IR system is never fully reliable. For example, it can identify a document as being relevant to the query, but a human expert would judge differently (*false positive*). Furthermore, a relevant document might not be found (*false negative*). The following table gives an overview of these possibilities.

		actual condition	
		is relevant	*is not relevant*
IR result	*is relevant*	true positive (tp)	false positive (fp)
	is not relevant	false negative (fn)	true negative (tn)

5.4.1 Precision, Recall, and Accuracy

The quality of an IR system can be measured by different criteria, e.g., the time needed to retrieve the answer set, the number of results, and the accuracy of the results. In this section, we focus on the relevancy of the results, i.e., of how precise the answer set is compared to the query.

Let R be the set of relevant documents, A the set of retrieved documents, Ra the retrieved and relevant documents so that $Ra = R \cap A$ and $|\cdot|$ the number of documents in a given set.

- The precision is the fraction of retrieved documents that are relevant:

$$Precision = \frac{|Ra|}{|A|} = \frac{tp}{tp + fp}. \tag{5.5}$$

- The recall is the fraction of relevant documents that are retrieved:

$$Recall = \frac{|Ra|}{|R|} = \frac{tp}{tp + fn}. \tag{5.6}$$

- The accuracy is the fraction of correct classifications:

$$Accuracy = \frac{tp + tn}{tp + fp + fn + tn}. \tag{5.7}$$

Example

For the sake of illustration, let us suppose that D is the set of all documents in the database and q a given query. Further, a group of human experts identified the set of documents R as being relevant to the query ($R \subseteq D$). The two sets have the following values:

$$D = \{d_1, d_2, d_3, d_4, d_5, d_6, d_7, d_8, d_9, d_{10}, d_{11}, d_{12}, d_{13}, d_{14}\},$$
$$R = \{d_2, d_4, d_6, d_7, d_{11}, d_{13}\}.$$

Here, $|R| = 6$ and remains constant. Now, let A be the set of documents that was identified by an IR system as being relevant to the query ($A \subseteq D$):

$$A = \{d_2, d_3, d_6, d_7, d_9, d_{10}, d_{11}, d_{12}, d_{13}\}.$$

The following table depicts the precision and recall at each iteration:

D	d_1	d_2	d_3	d_4	d_5	d_6	d_7	d_8	d_9	d_{10}	d_{11}	d_{12}	d_{13}	d_{14}
R		×		×		×	×				×		×	
A		×	×			×	×		×	×	×	×	×	
Ra		×				×	×				×		×	
$|A|$	0	1	2	2	2	3	4	4	5	6	7	8	9	9
$|Ra|$	0	1	1	1	1	2	3	3	3	3	4	4	5	5
precision	100%	100%	50%	50%	50%	67%	75%	75%	60%	50%	57%	50%	56%	0%
recall	0%	17%	17%	17%	17%	33%	50%	50%	50%	50%	67%	67%	83%	83%

The above table is to be interpreted like this:

- After the relevancy of document d_1 has been analyzed (a true negative), the precision is 100% and the recall is 0%. In deed, of all the documents analyzed so far, all the relevant documents were found (precision = 100%) and 0% of all the relevant documents were retrieved (recall).
- After document d_2 has been analyzed (a true positive), the precision remains at 100% and the recall rises to 17%. In deed, of all the documents analyzed so far, all the relevant documents were found (precision = 100%) and 17% of all the relevant documents were retrieved (recall).
- After document d_3 has been analyzed (a false positive), the precision falls to 50% and the recall remains at 17%. In deed, of all the documents analyzed so far, one out of two relevant documents were found (precision = 50%) and 17% of all the relevant documents were found (recall).
- ...
- The precision drops to 0 after the last relevant document has been analyzed (here: d_{13}).

In order to be able to compare different retrieval algorithms in terms of precision and recall, 11 *standard recall levels* are used: 0%, 10%, 20%, 30%, 40%, 50%, 60%, 70%, 80%, 90%, and 100%. Since the recall levels for each query might be distinct from the 11 standard recall levels, the utilization of an interpolation procedure is necessary. For example, let $r_j \in \{0, 1, 2, ..., 10\}$ be a reference to the jth standard recall level (i.e., r_5 is a reference to the recall level 5), then the precision for of the rth recall level is:

$$Precision(r_j) = max_{r_j \leq r \leq r_{j+1}} Precision(r).$$

Applied to the above table, this would result in:

recall	0%	10%	20%	30%	40%	50%	60%	70%	80%	90%	100%
precision	100%	100%	87,5%	66,7%	75%	60%	57%	28,5%	55,6%	0%	0%

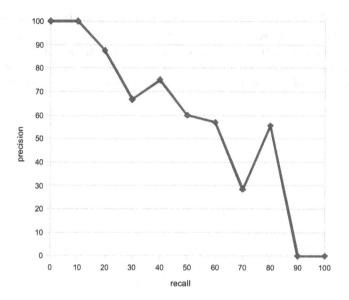

Fig. 5.7. Precision and recall.

The precision values for $r = 20\%$ and $r = 70\%$ have been averaged from their left and right neighboring values. Figure 5.7 shows the precision and recall with respect to the 11 standard recall levels. Generally, the precision curves fall with increasing recall.

Here is an overview of the quality of the retrieval:

| **correct** | true positives $\{d_2, d_6, d_7, d_{11}, d_{13}\}$ |
| | true negatives $\{d_1, d_5, d_8, d_{14}\}$ |

| **incorrect** | false positives $\{d_3, d_9, d_{10}, d_{12}\}$ |
| | false negatives $\{d_4\}$ |

Finally, the accuracy of the IR algorithm used in this example is:

$$accuracy = \frac{tp + tn}{tp + fp + fn + tn}$$
$$= \frac{5 + 4}{5 + 4 + 1 + 4}$$
$$= \frac{9}{14}$$
$$accuracy = 64\%$$

This chapter has highlighted the complex diversity that exists in the domain of IR. Research into IR is all the more important if we keep in mind the ever-growing resources represented by large and complex databases such as the WWW. Google's unrivaled rise in the domain of IR has clearly shown that in today's world, you are not a business leader if you merely have access to all the information that is available; you also need to be able to get the information you need the very moment you want it. Indeed, what is the use of a particular piece of information if you cannot access it quickly and efficiently?

Part II

Design and Utilization of E-Librarian Services

6

Ontological Approach

Multimedia content in electronic form is increasing dramatically in online and offline digital repositories. This raises the problem that there is too much unreliable, redundant, and irrelevant information. Finding appropriate answers is a rather difficult task, as it relies on the user filtering the pertinent information from the *noise*. Turning knowledge bases into useful resources requires identifying correct, reliable, and "machine-understandable" information, as well as developing simple but efficient search tools with the ability to reason over this information.

Fundamental techniques in knowledge representation, information retrieval, and natural language processing (NLP) have been presented in the first part of this book. In this second part, we provide details and suggestions on how to design an E-Librarian Service; an ontology-driven expert system.

6.1 Expert Systems

Computer applications that are able to explain their reasoning are commonly referred to as *expert systems*. An expert system employs knowledge about its application domain and uses logical reasoning services to solve problems that would otherwise require human competence or expertise. Such specific systems rely on a specialized knowledge base and a specific inference engine.

6.1.1 Classical Expert Systems

Classical expert systems work by deductive reasoning based on a set of propositions or rules. Each rule is of the form:

if *antecedent*, then *consequent*

written:

$$p \rightarrow q.$$

Deductive reasoning starts with generalizations and arrives at more specific knowledge. *Inductive reasoning* takes specific knowledge and makes generalizations.

There are two methods of reasoning in expert systems: forward chaining and backward chaining. *Forward chaining* starts with the available data and searches the rules until it finds one in which the antecedent is known to be true. It then adds the consequent to its data and continues to do this until a goal has been reached. *Backward chaining* starts with a goal and searches the rules until it finds one which has a consequent that matches the goal. If the antecedent for that rule is true, then it is added to the list of goals.

The following example illustrates deductive reasoning through a set of old farmer rules. The aim is to calculate if this year's harvest will be good. The knowledge base of the expert system contains 5 rules, R1 to R5, as shown in the following table.

Rule	Antecedent	Consequent
R1	if the winter is rigorous,	then there will be a lot of snow in February
R2	if the year is divisible by 7,	then it will freeze in May
R3	if the swallows leave early in autumn,	then winter will be rigorous
R4	if it freezes in May,	then harvest will be bad
R5	if there is a lot of snow in February,	then harvest will be good

Let us suppose that the user would like to know if harvest will be good this year. In a backward chaining process, the reasoning engine identifies rule R5 as being able to deliver the answer to the user's question, but only if the systems has the information if there was a lot of snow in February. The answer to that question can be determined with rule R1. But here, the missing information is whether the winter was rigorous. Rule R3 can provide the answer, but it needs to know if the swallows left early this year. This information cannot be found in the knowledge base and there is no other rule that can provide an answer to this question. Therefore, the system has to ask the user for input.

```
USER: Will harvest be good?
SYSTEM: Did the swallows leave early in autumn?
USER: Yes.
SYSTEM: Yes, harvest will be good.
```

This kind of reasoning is generally known as *weak artificial intelligence*; the machine is able to come to a certain conclusion by inferring over implicit knowledge and by applying some defined rules.

Since the 1990s, ontologies have been used in such expert systems by the insight that they provide a significant added value. It is through the Semantic

Web movement that ontologies have considerably gained in importance (see section 2.2).

6.1.2 Ontology-Driven Expert Systems

It is widely agreed that ontologies will play a key role in modern expert systems, particularly in the field of knowledge management and digital libraries. The most important advantage of such systems is that their data is organized in an ontological way, i.e., in terms of concepts, attributes, and individuals. Complementary to reasoning services, such as those used in "classical" expert systems, ontology-driven expert systems have a broader variety of inferencing procedures over the knowledge base (see section 3.4). For example, as the data is organized in a hierarchical way, more general or more specific expressions can be inferred.

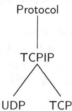

Fig. 6.1. hierarchy of concepts.

For illustration purposes, let us consider an expert system that provides an online help-desk about computer networks with a knowledge base that is organized in a ontological way, as shown in figure 6.1. The ontology defines the concept Protocol as the super-concept of the concept TCPIP. The latter has the two sub-concepts TCP and UDP. Furthermore, let us suppose that the system has a set of four rules, R1 to R4, as shown in the following table.

Rule	Antecedent	Consequent
R1	if it is a network,	then it requires a protocol
R2	if the Internet is to be used,	then TCP/IP is required
R3	if video streaming is to be used,	then UDP is required
R4	if a file is to be transferred,	then TCP is required

For example, a user would like to know if he needs to install the TCP/IP protocol on his computer if he wants to watch streaming video over the Internet. Rule R3 is about video streaming. However, the consequent does not match against TCP/IP, because it is about UDP, but there is no other rule about this topic. By logical reasoning over its knowledge base, the inference engine can conclude that UDP is a specialization of TCP/IP and can thus provide an answer to the user's question.

```
USER: Do I need TCP/IP on my computer for video-streaming?
SYSTEM: Yes.
SYSTEM: The TCP/IP sub-protocol UDP will be used.
```

Examples of Related Systems

ontology-driven expert systems exist for nearly every domain of application. Here are some examples of such systems.

- The prototype PRECISE uses ontology technology to map semantically tractable NL questions to the corresponding SQL query [Pop05].
- An ontology-driven semantic search is presented in [BCFB04] that allows to set up semantic level relevance feedback for query concept focalization, generalization, etc.
- *OntoNova* is an ontology-based question-answering system in chemistry [AMO+03]. The system is able to logically infer over the domain specific knowledge base and to justify its answers giving NL explanations.
- A domain ontology information retrieval system based on speech recognition is presented in [TGF+07].
- A system for reasoning over multimedia E-Learning objects is described in [EHLS06]. Here, a speech recognition engine is used for keyword spotting. It extracts the taxonomy node that corresponds to the keyword, and associates it to the multimedia objects as metadata.

6.2 Towards an E-Librarian Service

6.2.1 Reasoning Capabilities of an E-Librarian Service

An E-Librarian Service is able to retrieve multimedia resources from a knowledge base in a more efficient way than by browsing through an index or by using a simple keyword search. The premise is that more pertinent results would be retrieved if the *semantic search engine* "understood" the sense of the user query and were able to reason over the data. The returned results would then be logical consequences of an inference rather than of keyword matchings.

An E-Librarian Service does not return the answer to the user question, but it retrieves the most pertinent document(s) in which the user finds the answer to his question. For example, let us suppose that the user asked the following question:

$$What\ are\ the\ tasks\ of\ a\ protocol? \qquad (6.1)$$

The E-Librarian Service would then deliver a document in which the user finds the answer to his question. The librarian approach of solving complex retrieval problems has already been discussed in section 1.3.4.

An E-Librarian Service is an ontology driven expert system about a given domain, e.g., computer history, fractions in mathematics, or networks in computer science. It relies on specialized and hierarchically organized knowledge bases, and specific reasoning services. The documents in the knowledge base are described by metadata that is encoded in a knowledge representation formalism, like the *Web Ontology Language* (OWL).

The ontological approach of designing an E-Librarian Service is also helpful to resolve ambiguities in the NL user question, like multiple sense words. Let us consider as an illustration the word "Ada", which can refer to the programming language named "Ada", but which can also be the name of the person "Augusta Ada Lovelace". The correct interpretation can only be retrieved accurately by putting the ambiguous word in the context of a complete question. Let us consider the following questions:

$$Who\ invented\ Ada?\qquad(6.2)$$

$$Did\ the\ companies\ Bull\ and\ Honeywell\ create\ Ada?'\qquad(6.3)$$

The context of these two questions reveals that here "Ada" is the programming language and not the person "Ada". The resolution of ambiguities will be explained in section 7.3.3.

6.2.2 Deploying an Ontology

An ontology plays a key role in an E-Librarian Service. It is used for different purposes.

- The documents in the knowledge base are semantically described with metadata. This metadata uses a vocabulary that is defined in the ontology. A vocabulary contains concepts, roles, and individuals that are organized in a hierarchical way. The metadata is serialized in a machine-readable form, e.g., as OWL/XML (see section 6.3).
- The user can enter his question in NL. This allows the user to communicate with the system in a simple, but efficient way. For the semantic interpretation of the user question, i.e., the translation from NL into a machine-readable form, the ontology is used to map NL words to ontology concepts and roles (see chapter 7).
- The E-Librarian Service's semantic search engine is able to logically infer over the knowledge base and the user question in order to use implicit knowledge. In this way, the user question can be generalized or specialized and put in the appropriated context, which eventually results in fewer, but more pertinent documents that are retrieved (see chapter 8).

Example

For illustration purposes, let us consider a digital library about university lectures, like the online tele-TASK archive. A basic idea is to split recorded lectures into smaller *clips* with the idea that users generally ask short and precise questions and expect short and precise answers. They prefer short clips with a length of some minutes to complete lectures of 90 minutes. Such an E-Librarian Service will be presented in more details in section 10.3.

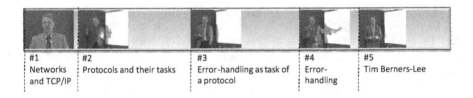

Fig. 6.2. Semantic decomposition of a video.

Figure 6.2 depicts a fictional representation of an university lecture. It is split into 5 different clips. Each clip is about a precise topic, as shown in the following table.

Clip	Description
#1	information about computer networks and TCP/IP
#2	information about protocols and their tasks
#3	explanation that error-handling is a task of a protocol
#4	explanation on how error-handling works
#5	explantation that Tim Berners-Lee (co-)invented the WWW

Each clip can now be described in a formal way, i.e., through Description Logics (DL), as explained in chapters 2 and 3. Clip #3 could be described as follows:

$$\text{Clip3} \equiv \text{Protocol} \sqcap \exists \text{hasTask}.\text{ErrorHandling}. \tag{6.4}$$

Finally, the above expression could be serialized in a machine-readable form using a knowledge representation formalism, like OWL/XML. The listing shown in figure 6.3 contains, in addition to the formal translation of the above DL-concept description (6.4), metadata about the topic of the clip (`rdfs:label`) as well as a link to the physical video document (`demo:filename`), and the start- and end-time of the clip inside the complete video (`demo:startTime` and `demo:endTime`).

Let us suppose that the user enters the question shown in (6.1). Obviously, he does not exactly know what he is looking for, e.g., he does not know that error-handling is a task of a protocol. Thus, it is important that the expert system "understand" the meaning of the question and yields only semantically

```
<owl:Class rdf:about="Clip3">
  <rdfs:label>
    A protocol is able to handle errors during transmission
  </rdfs:label>
  <demo:startTime>00:42:00,56</demo:startTime>
  <demo:endTime>00:43:52,80</demo:endTime>
  <demo:filename>lectureWWW\www12.smil</demo:filename>
  <rdfs:subClassOf rdf:resource="#Protocol" />
  <rdfs:subClassOf>
    <owl:Restriction>
      <owl:onProperty rdf:resource="#hasTask" />
      <owl:someValuesFrom rdf:resource="#Error_Handling" />
    </owl:Restriction>
  </rdfs:subClassOf>
</owl:Class>
```

Fig. 6.3. OWL/XML serialization of metadata.

relevant answers, such as clip #3 in our example. For the same question, a classical keyword-based search engine might have retrieved documents in which the words "protocol" and "task" occurred, as with clip #2; however, this would not be the best possible answer. The way in which the inference engine of an E-Librarian Service works in detail will be the subject of the next chapters.

6.2.3 Designing the Ontological Background

The design and realization of an ontology requires important resources and have to be done with a maximum of care as it is the sole part of the final system. As a result, *ontological engineering* has gained major importance in the recent years.

Ontology engineering, in analogy to software engineering, is concerned with the challenges of designing ontologies by providing methodologies and tools for their development, evaluation, and maintenance.

A major goal in ontological engineering is to create specialized domain ontologies for every imaginable topic. The Linked Data initiative suggests to use existing ontologies and controlled vocabularies as far as possible (see section 2.2.3).

Qualitative ontologies for different domains emerge every week, for very specialized, or novel, domains. However, there are reasons why a developer of an E-Librarian Service has to design a new ontology, e.g., because there is no ontology about that domain yet. Existing ontologies may not be optimized for one's needs. They may lack expressiveness, so that one wants to add supplementary features to have a more precise and pertinent ontology.

The level of granularity of an ontology is also a topic of concern. On the one hand, the more detailed the taxonomy is, the more exactly the system can classify the documents and infer over the user question. On the other hand, a very detailed taxonomy reduces the tolerance of the NL processing; the user questions must be correctly and precisely formulated.

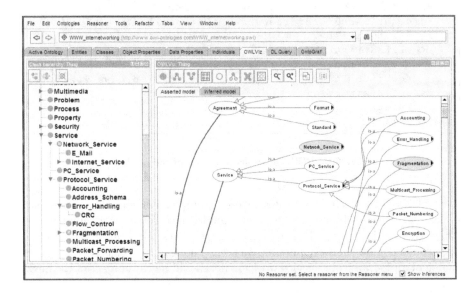

Fig. 6.4. The tool *Protégé* and an ontology about networks in computer science.

Most ontologies are designed using tools or editors like Protégé[1] [KFNM04], as depicted in figure 6.4, OntoSutdio[2], or KAON2[3]. An overview of 140 ontology tools can be found here: [Ber10]. As this book is not about ontology engineering, we refer the interested reader to more specialized literature, e.g., [SS04, HKR10, BCT07, Haf10, GPCGFL03, RDH⁺04].

6.3 Semantic Annotation of the Knowledge Base

The creation of semantic annotation of documents is not and should not be the task of the user; nor should it be the task of the author of the document. The user and the author are not necessarily computer science experts who know how to create metadata in a specific formalism, like XML, RDF, or OWL. Furthermore, the creation of metadata is a subjective task and should

---

[1] http://protege.stanford.edu/

[2] http://www.ontoprise.de/en/home/products/ontostudio/

[3] http://kaon2.semanticweb.org/

be done conscientiously. The construction of sufficient metadata is a crucial element in the management and sustenance of digital repositories, libraries, and archives. In this section, we provide an overview of computer-assisted tools to create metadata as well as current techniques of automatic extraction and generation of metadata.

6.3.1 Computer-Assisted Creation of metadata

In order to assure that an E-Librarian Service relies on the most precise and concise metadata, one can decide to manually create an optimal annotation of the documents with respect to a given domain ontology. This task can be simplified by using a tool which offers the following services.

- A domain language is created. A list of all relevant words that are used in the documents is generated. They are extracted from the contents of the various documents. For example, if slides are used, then converting tools[4] can be used to extract their textual content. Similar software also exists for the conversion of pdf-files. The extracted words are then transformed into their lemmatized (canonical) form and duplicates are deleted. Here is an example of a domain language:

$$language=\{protocol, task, error\text{-}handling, invent\}$$

- The lemmatized words are classified into the ontology. Words that are not relevant for the given domain are ignored, i.e., *stop words*. The result of this classification is a domain dictionary, e.g.,

$$dictionary = \{ (\text{``protocol''},\text{Protocol}),(\text{``task''},\text{Task}),$$
$$(\text{``error-handling''},\text{ErrorHandling}),(\text{``invent''},\text{toInvent})\}$$

More details about domain language and domain dictionary are given in chapter 7.

- For each document in the knowledge base and for each sub-part of a document, e.g., a clip or a paragraph, a DL-concept description is formulated that best describes the content of the document. Based on the content of the document, the tool suggests pertinent concepts and roles from the domain dictionary and assists the user with their assembly into a valid DL-concept description, e.g.,

$$\text{Clip3} \equiv \text{Protocol} \sqcap \exists \text{hasTask.ErrorHandling}.$$

- Finally, in a fully automated process, this DL-concept description is serialized as an OWL/XML file as shown in figure 6.3.

---

[4] http://www.linckels.lu/logiciels/ppt2txt.zip

6.3.2 Automatic Generation of metadata

Although the manual creation of metadata is a labour intensive process, the automatic generation of reliable metadata is still a very difficult problem and currently a topic of ongoing research. In this section, we provide an overview of different approaches about the extraction of metadata from documents and about the automatic generation of semantic annotation for documents. Many of the existing approaches rely primarily on content analysis.

Natural Language Processing

When systems have to deal with text documents, NLP methods have proven effective in the extraction and classification of documents and terms within documents. *Information extraction* ranges from simple token analysis and part-of-speech tagging to full syntactic parsing (see chapter 4).

A first stage of information extraction is to determine index terms, i.e., words that stand for the context of the document. The aim is to identify particular patterns, such as the title or details about the author, or topics and genres. A second stage is to determine the relationships between such terms, also called *relationship extraction*.

Information extraction is heavily used by Web robots, crawlers, and agents. These tools browse the Web with the only task to index Web pages and documents with relevant index terms and metadata. The advantage of information extraction in Web pages is that the structure of the document can be used to extract supplementary semantics, such as headings expressed with the <h1>-tag.

Different techniques can be used to index documents, e.g., reading the HTML meta-tag values in case of Web pages, indexing frequent words, or performing more advanced NLP operations, such as tagging and parsing. Furthermore, external sources, e.g, dictionaries and thesauruses, can be used to group semantically equivalent words.

Collaborative Tagging

Tagging is the act of annotating documents, e.g., Web pages, images, and videos, with keywords called *tags* that are created on the fly by users. Basically, tagging allows users to express their opinions on how the digital library should be organized.

Instead of user-defined keywords, some systems provide a set of defined attributes which a user can use for tagging. In either way, the system can analyze how many documents share the same common attributes or keywords. Tags that have been agreed on by the majority of the users can be used to create metadata.

The problem with "classical tagging" is that tags have little or no value on their own and they certainly are not understood by computers. They are just strings denoting some type of concept. Such tags do not provide enough semantics to allow computer systems to generate reliable metadata. Tags are isolated words without relationships between them.

As more and more users participate and contribute to collaborative tagging, a new form of classification scheme emerges that is now commonly referred to as a folksonomy, a portmanteau of "folk" and "taxonomy". Folksonomies represent a bottom-up approach to annotating and organizing documents that is focused on and driven by end users. As such, they are structurally different from formal, top-down categorization schemes such as ontologies or taxonomies.

New ways of tagging, such as "semantic tagging", are based on defining tags as objects and not as keywords. These objects are linked, e.g., by using structured knowledge sources such as ontologies or thesauruses. Semantics could be attached to tags by mapping them to ontology concepts and roles. Technically, tagging metadata is represented in a formalism such as RDF and is thus available to semantic search and reasoning services.

Pattern Recognition and Classification

Pattern recognition is a field of machine learning which aims to give a kind of label to some data. Classification is the most common form of pattern recognition. For example, a document has to be classified into one category. This requires that the machine detect the sense of the document. If all documents are about sports, then categorization could be to label each document with the appropriate kind of sport, such as soccer or basketball.

Another popular example of pattern recognition are spam filters. Incoming e-mail is scanned for some known patterns that can be found in the content. The e-mail is then categorized ass "spam" or "non-spam". Pattern recognition is also used in many other areas, like part-of-speech tagging and speech recognition.

Pattern recognition algorithms generally aim to provide a reasonable answer for all possible inputs and to do "fuzzy" matching of inputs. This is opposed to pattern matching algorithms, which look for exact matches in the input with pre-existing patterns. Many common pattern recognition algorithms are probabilistic in nature, in the sense that they use statistical inference to find the best label for a given instance. Unlike other algorithms, which simply output a "best" label, probabilistic algorithms often also output a probability of the instance being described by the given label.

Use of Audio Data

The automatic semantic annotation of video documents is one of the biggest challenges in computer science. There is a broad range of techniques that are explored, e.g., image recognition, motion detection, and speech recognition. A particular field of interest is the annotation and indexing of television shows.

Advances in speech recognition software make audio data a promising source of potential metadata. Instead of merely keywords being extracted, terms from an audio transcript can be mapped to ontology concepts and then ranked according their relevance, e.g., their frequency of occurrence inside the document. In this way, only the concepts with highest frequency are used as metadata. Experiments have shown that the quality of generated metadata from audio information is sufficient for an E-Librarian Service.

Unlike other machine learning techniques, the use of audio data has at least two specific weaknesses. Firstly, the quality of the speech recognition software is a primary factor. For example, if the audio was recorded in a room with bad acoustics, then the transcript may contain many errors and make it unusable. The quality of the transcript gets even worse when the speech recognition system is not well trained for a particular speaker. Secondly, NL in general is often a source of linguistic ambiguities, especially if a more specialized vocabulary is used. For example, different people pronounce domain specific words differently, like the German word "Mann", which can mean "a man" (German: "Mann"), but it can also mean "one" (German: "man"), or a network "MAN" (Metropolitan Area Network). All three are pronounced in a similar way.

Combinations of Different Techniques

There is still no reliable technique for the automatic extraction and generation of metadata. However, different techniques, like the ones cited above, can be helpful for suggesting a first draft of annotations, especially when dealing with large knowledge bases.

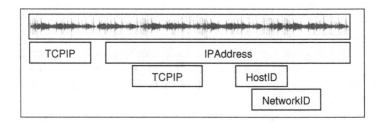

Fig. 6.5. Example of overlapping concepts.

Furthermore, the combination of different techniques can be complementary and improve the process of creating semantic annotations, e.g., by comparing audio and textual data to identify overlapping areas. In in figure 6.5, the speaker uses the expression "host ID" (audio data) in a certain part of the presentation and simultaneously shows a slide with the term "host ID" (textual data). Because the same term is used in both sources of information at the same time, the concept HostID is relevant in the context of this document, and more important than a word that was only found in one of both data sources (audio or slide).

A novel approach is to divide multimedia documents into cohesive areas of accumulated appearance of an equal word [Rep09]. For example, in the space of five minutes, the speaker used the expression "host ID" three times. This segment of five minutes is called a *chain* about the concept HostID.

A chain is always about one specific word. Chains overlap when the speaker uses different relevant words several times during the same time interval. The resulting granularity of the segmentation depends on the allowed *gap* between two identical words. An improvement of this approach is to give a weight to chains, e.g., if a word appears very often in a chain, then that chain has more weight than a chain where this word appears less frequently.

7

Design of the Natural Language Processing Module

An E-Librarian Service allows users to enter complete questions in natural language (NL) in order to improve the retrieval capabilities (see section 1.3.3). The aim of the natural language processing (NLP) module of an E-Librarian Service is to translate a user question into a logical and computer-readable form. The more precise and accurate this translation is, the more complex the algorithm gets. In this chapter we present the necessary principles to design the NLP module of an E-Librarian Service that is able to "understand" the meaning of a user question and to translate it into a logical form.

7.1 Overview of the Semantic Interpretation

7.1.1 Logical Form

The process of translating an NL sentence, i.e., a user question, into a logical form is called *semantic interpretation* (see section 4.6). An E-Librarian Service is based on Description Logics (DL) as knowledge representation language (see chapter 3).

First, DL have the advantage that they come with well-defined semantics and inference services. Second, the link between DL and NL has already been established [Sch93, Fra03]. Third, an E-Librarian Service uses Semantic Web technologies like the Web Ontology Language (OWL) to structure its knowledge base, and DL are the formal semantics of OWL (see chapter 6). Thus, DL are the common knowledge representation language for serializing metadata and for interpreting user questions.

Before explaining in detail how the semantic interpretation works, we will illustrate the principles of the NLP module with two examples. Let us suppose that the user enters the following questions in NL:

$$Who\ invented\ TCP/IP? \tag{7.1}$$

$$\textit{What are the tasks of a protocol?} \tag{7.2}$$

The semantic interpretation of both questions could result in the following logical forms, i.e., DL-concept descriptions:

- for question in (7.1): Person $\sqcap$ ∃invent.TCPIP,
- for question in (7.2): Thing $\sqcap$ ∃taskOf.Protocol.

7.1.2 Processing of a User Question

The semantic interpretation is divided into three steps as shown in figure 7.1. In the NLP pre-processing, the tokens from the user query are identified and transformed into their canonical form. This task is called *lemmatization*. Tokens that have not been recognized, i.e., words that were not found in the domain dictionary, are processed separately. These can be misspelled words or simply words that are not yet in the domain dictionary.

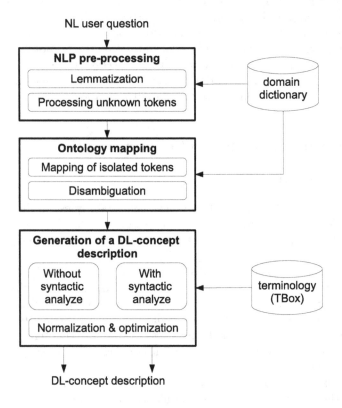

Fig. 7.1. Representation of the semantic interpretation of a NL user question.

Secondly, each token from the user question is mapped to one or more ontology concepts or roles. The disambiguation of possible multiple-sense words is a separate task.

Thirdly, a DL-concept description is generated that represents the meaning of the user question. The syntax of the NL sentence can be analyzed to create a more accurate translation of the user question. Finally, the resulting logical form is optimized and normalized.

7.2 NLP Pre-Processing

The NLP pre-processing consists of two task: the lemmatization of the user question and the processing of words that cannot be found in the domain dictionary.

7.2.1 Domain Language

It is expected that the use of a controlled vocabulary leads to an improvement of the retrieval performance [BYRN99]. Expert systems are generally dedicated to a specific domain, e.g., networks in computer science, or fractions in mathematics. Obviously, an E-Librarian Service should have a rich vocabulary about the given domain.

The *domain language* contains verbs, nouns, articles, proper names, numbers, etc. The same domain language can contain words in different languages. The multi-language feature of an E-Librarian Service is explained in section 7.6. An example of a language for the domain of computer networks is:

L_H = {who, invent, tcpip, what, be, the, task, protocol, error-handling}.

Definition 7.1 (domain language). *Let L be the set of all existing words over a certain alphabet that might be used to formulate a query, so that $L \subseteq \Sigma^*$. A domain language L_H is the set of all words that are known in a given domain, so that $L_H \subseteq L \subseteq \Sigma^*$.*

7.2.2 Lemmatization

A user question is a string of words. Generally, each word can be considered as one token. However, in some cases, a token can be composed of several words; "hard drive" can be processed as one token. The detection of tokens and the transformation into their canonical form (*lemma*), as explained in section 4.2.2, is called *lemmatization*. Each lemma belongs to a certain word category, such as verb, noun, article, and so on.

This particular task of the linguistic pre-processing is commonly performed by a *part-of-speech (POS) tagger*. A list of taggers is given in appendix D. Most POS taggers are based on statistical observations and trained over large corpora. For different implementations, we used *TreeTagger*, which is a lightweight, reliable, and easy-to-use tagger. The authors[1] also granted us permission to modify the dictionary so that we could adapt it to our needs.

7.2.3 Handling Spelling Errors

Systems that allow users to freely enter sentences in NL have to have a certain tolerance against spelling errors. If a misspelled or unknown word is encountered, the system has to compute to which known word in the domain language it would fit best.

Most commonly, the mechanism of computing the similarity of words, known as *similarity-based generalization*, is used for the processing of unknown words. It states that a system automatically acquires a relative measure of how similar a new word is to known words. Several algorithms are available like the *Levenshtein function* (see section 4.2.4).

Definition 7.2 (word equivalence). *The function $\pi(a, b)$ quantifies the similarity of two given words a and b in a language L, so that a and b are said to be equivalent with respect to a given tolerance ε, written $a \equiv b$, iff $\pi(a, b) \leq \varepsilon$.*

$$\textit{What are the tasXks of a protocol?}^* \tag{7.3}$$

For the question in (7.3), the E-Librarian Service is able to compute the similarity of the token "tasXks" to the word "task" from the domain language. The following table illustrates the use of the word equivalency as defined in 7.2:

a	b	ε	$\pi(a, b)$	$a \equiv^? b$
task	tasXks	0	2	$a \not\equiv b$
task	tasXks	1	3	$a \equiv b$
task	tasXks	2	3	$a \equiv b$
task	asXks	2	4	$a \not\equiv b$
task	asXks	3	3	$a \equiv b$

7.3 Ontology Mapping

The result of the NLP pre-processing is a list of lemmatized tokens. Now, the principle is to map each token to one or more concepts in the ontology and to handle possible ambiguities in the interpretation of words, i.e., multiple-sense words.

---

[1] Helmut Schmid and Sabine Schulte im Walde, Institut für Machinelle Sprachverarbeitung (IMS), University of Stuttgart.

7.3.1 Domain Dictionary

An E-Librarian Service uses a dictionary, thesaurus, or other structured repository to compute the relations between words in terms of hyperonym, hyponym, synonym, and homonyms (see section 4.3.1). A popular example of such a resource is *WordNet*[2] [Ma98].

The semantics are attached to each word in the domain language by classification in a *domain dictionary*. It is structured in a hierarchical way and represents relationships between words as described above.

Definition 7.3 (domain dictionary). *A domain dictionary $H = (V, E, v_0)$ is a rooted and oriented tree, where each node except the root-node (v_0), has one or more parents. A node represents a concept in an ontology. E is the set of all edges and V is the set of all nodes (vertices) with $V = \{(s, T)|s \in S\}$, where s is a unique identifier and T is a set of words from the domain language that are associated to a node, so that $T = \{t|t \in L_H\}$.*

Concept: TCPIP
$s = $ **demo:TCPIP**
$T = \{$tcp/ip, tcpip, tcp-ip$\}$

Role: invent
$s = $ **demo:invent**
$T = \{$invent, build, create$\}$

Fig. 7.2. The nodes representing the concept TCPIP and the role invent.

A node v in the domain dictionary represents a *concept* or *role* in the ontology. The words that refer to a concept are regrouped in T. We assume that each set of words T_i is semantically related to the concept that the node v_i represents. Figure 7.2 illustrates this idea with the words "tcp/ip", "tcpip", and "tcp-ip" that refer to the same concept TCPIP. Also, the role invent is referred to by the words "invent", "build", and "create". This means that the two following sentences are semantically identical after lemmatization and according to the above domain dictionary:

$$Who\ invented\ TCPIP? \qquad (7.4)$$

$$Who\ created\ TCP\text{-}IP? \qquad (7.5)$$

7.3.2 Mapping of Words

The mapping returns a set of valid interpretations for a given word. In this way, semantically irrelevant words (*stop words*) are filtered out. According to Zipf's law (see section 4.1.3), a stop list with a few dozen words can optimize the semantic interpretation considerably.

---

[2] http://wordnet.princeton.edu/

A word is *semantically relevant* if there is at least one interpretation (concept or role) in the domain dictionary. An ambiguity is detected if the mapping returns more than one interpretation. The resolution of such ambiguities is explained in section 7.3.3.

The mapping of the word w is written $\varphi(w)$ and $|\varphi(w)|$ stands for the number of items returned by the mapping. The result of a mapping has to be interpreted as follows:

$$|\varphi(w)| \begin{cases} = 0 & w \text{ is a stop word and will be ignored} \\ = 1 & w \text{ was successfully mapped} \\ > 1 & w \text{ is a multiple-sense word and requires disambiguation} \end{cases}$$

For the sake of simplicity, we suppose that the examples provided in this section do not create ambiguities. The following mapping uses the nodes from the domain dictionary as depicted in figure 7.2.

$$\varphi(\text{"tcp-ip"}) = \{\text{TCPIP}\}$$
$$\varphi(\text{"tcp/ip"}) = \{\text{TCPIP}\}$$
$$\varphi(\text{"the"}) = \{\}$$
$$\varphi(\text{"built"}) = \{\text{invent}\}$$
$$\varphi(\text{"invent"}) = \{\text{invent}\}$$

Fig. 7.3. Examples of the mapping of lemmatized words.

Figure 7.3 shows some examples of mappings where all words except "the" are semantically relevant. The example illustrates that the words "tcp-ip" and "tcp/ip" are mapped to the same ontology concept TCPIP. Also, the words "build" and "invent" are mapped to the same ontology role invent.

Lemma	Word category	Ontology concept
who	WP	concept: Person
invent	VBP	role: invent
tcpip	NP	concept: TCPIP

Table 7.1. Mapping of the question: "Who invented TCP/IP?"

To provide a full example of the NLP pre-processing and the mapping of words, let us consider the questions in (7.1) and (7.2). The result of the mappings is depicted in tables 7.1 and 7.2.

Lemma	Word category	Ontology concept
what	WP	concept: Thing
be	VBP	$\top$
the	DT	$\top$
task	NNS	role: hasTask
of	IN	$\top$
a	DT	$\top$
protocol	NP	concept: Protocol

Table 7.2. Mapping of the question: "What are the tasks of a protocol?"

Definition 7.4 (mapping). *The meaning of a word $w \in L$ is made explicit with the mapping function $\varphi : L \to V$ over a domain language L_H with respect to a domain dictionary $H = (V, E, v_0)$, so that $\varphi(w)$ returns a set of interpretations defined as follows,*

$$\varphi(w) = \{v_i | \exists x \in ft(v_i) : w \equiv x\}.$$

The function $ft(v_i)$ returns the set of words T_i associated to the node v_i and $w \equiv x$ are two equivalent words according to a given tolerance regarding spelling errors (see definition 7.2).

7.3.3 Resolving Ambiguities

Some words in NL have different meanings or senses. If these words are used outside a specific context, there is an *ambiguity* about how they must be interpreted. For example, the word "date" may refer to "a social or romantic appointment or engagement" or to "a sweet, dark brown, oval fruit containing a hard stone, often eaten dried".

The task of *disambiguation* or resolving ambiguities, is to determine which of the senses of an ambiguous word is invoked in a particular use of the word. Heuristic algorithms for word-sense disambiguation generally analyze the context of the use of the word.

Detection of Ambiguities

It is possible that a word can be mapped to different ontology concepts at once, so that $|\varphi(w)| > 1$. In that case, we call w a multiple-sense word.

An example of a multiple-sense word is depicted in figure 7.4, where the word "Ada" can refer to the person *Augusta Ada Lovelace* or to the programming language *Ada*. As a matter of fact, the mapping of the word "Ada" causes an ambiguity because:

$$\varphi(\text{``}Ada\text{''}) = \{\text{Ada\_Person, Ada\_Language}\}.$$

An ambiguous word is detected when the mapping function returns more than one possible interpretation.

Concept: Ada_Person
$s = $ demo:Ada_Person
$T = $ {ada}

Concept: Ada_Language
$s = $ demo:Ada_Language
$T = $ {ada}

Fig. 7.4. The two nodes for the multiple-sense word "Ada".

Focusing on the Context

The notion of *focus* solves this problem, which is based on the principle of *semantic filtering using selectional restrictions*. The focus is the function f, which returns the best interpretation for a given word in the context of the complete user question. The task of the algorithm is to make a forced choice between the different senses of the ambiguous word based on the context of use.

The focus extends the definition of a node in the domain dictionary (see section 7.2.1) by adding to each role two additional properties (arg_1 and arg_2) which specify the *role's signature*.

A role r has the signature $r(arg_1, arg_2)$, where arg_1 and arg_2 are two identifiers (see definition 7.3). The signature of each role defines the kind of arguments that are possible.

Role: invent
$s = $ demo:invent
$T = $ {invent, build, create}
$arg_1 = $ demo:Person
$arg_2 = $ demo:Thing

Fig. 7.5. The role invent with its signature.

Figure 7.5 illustrates the the role invent(Person, Thing), which is the role $r = $ invent that has the arguments $arg_1 = $ Person and $arg_2 = $ Thing. It stands for: "Somebody invented something." To illustrate the principle of disambiguation, let us consider the following question:

$$\textit{Who invented Ada?} \hspace{3cm} (7.6)$$

For the above question, the following mappings would be computed:

$$\varphi(\text{"who"}) = \{\text{Person}\}$$
$$\varphi(\text{"invent"}) = \{\text{invent(Person}, \textbf{Thing})\}$$
$$\varphi(\text{"ada"}) = \{\text{Ada\_Person, Ada\_Language}\}$$

The system detects an ambiguity for the word "Ada", which is mapped to both the concept Ada_Person and the concept Ada_Language. Let us also suppose that the system uses the following terminology as explained in section 3.2:

$$Person \sqsubseteq \top$$
$$Thing \sqsubseteq \top$$
$$Person \equiv \neg Thing$$
$$Who \sqsubseteq Person$$
$$Ada\_Person \sqsubseteq Person$$
$$Ada\_Language \sqsubseteq Thing$$

In order to solve the ambiguity, the system computes and verifies all possible combinations, which are:

- invent(Person, **Ada_Person**)
  This combination is excluded knowing that $Ada\_Person \not\sqsubseteq Thing$.

- invent(Person, **Ada_Language**)
  This combination is valid because $Ada\_Language \sqsubseteq Thing$.

Finally, the correct result of the focus function is:

$$f(\varphi(\text{"Ada"})) = Ada\_Language.$$

Thus, the system will process the user question as being:

$$Who\ invented\ the\ programming\ language\ Ada? \tag{7.7}$$

The correct semantic interpretation would be:

$$Person \sqcap \exists invent.Ada\_Language. \tag{7.8}$$

Technically, the signature of each role is defined in the ontology using the RDFS-elements **range** and **domain**, as shown in the following example for the role invent:

```
<owl:ObjectProperty rdf:about="&demo;invent">
  <rdfs:isDefinedBy rdf:resource="&demo;" />
  <rdfs:domain rdf:resource="&demo;Thing" />
  <rdfs:range rdf:resource="&demo;Person" />
</owl:ObjectProperty>
```

Definition 7.5 (focus). *The interpretation of a mapping $\varphi(w)$ in the context of a given question q is made explicit by the function f. The focus, written $f_q(\varphi(w)) = v'$, guarantees the following:*

1. *$v' \in \varphi(w)$; the focused word is a valid interpretation,*
2. *$|f_q(\varphi(w))| = [0,1]$; the focus function returns 0 or 1 result,*
3. *$\top \leq v' \leq \bot$, iff $f_q(\varphi(w)) \neq \emptyset$; if the focusing is successful, then the word is semantically related to the domain of the ontology,*
4. *$(\exists x \in ft(v'), \forall y \in ft(v_i \in \varphi(w)))\ \pi(w,x) \geq \pi(w,y)$, iff $f_q(\varphi(w)) \neq \emptyset$; if the focussing is successful, then the returned interpretation contains the best matching word of all possible interpretations.*

Limitations and Constraints

It is still possible that the focus function cannot resolve an ambiguity, e.g., a given word has more interpretations, but the focus function returns an empty set. In such a case, the system could generate a DL-concept description for each possible interpretation. This would result in separate queries for each context of interpretation.

Other formulations in NL that cause ambiguities are possible. For example, a word has different word categories, such as the word "blink", which can be a noun (a blink of the eye) or a verb (to blink). Such situations can be resolved with the algorithm described above.

Finally, from practical experience we know that users generally enter simple questions where the disambiguation is successful. If word categories for disambiguation, as suggested here, are used, an accuracy of 90% is easy to achieve [MS99].

7.4 Generation of a DL-Concept Description

The generation of a DL-concept description that best reproduces the semantics of the user question depends on the complexity of the interpretation algorithm and the complexity of the used DL-language. In this section, we describe and discuss the benefits of syntactic analysis for the semantic interpretation.

7.4.1 Without Syntactic Analysis

If the syntax of the user question is not considered, then the semantic interpretation is simply the conjunction of the identified concepts and roles (see section 7.3.2):

$$Q = \prod_{k=1}^{n} \varphi(w \in q)$$

where n is the number of words in the question q. The order of the concepts and roles as they appear in a DL-concept description is not important.

Examples

The question shown in (7.1) with its mapping depicted in table 7.1 could be translated into the following DL-concept description:

$$Q \equiv \mathsf{Person} \sqcap \exists \mathsf{invent} \sqcap \mathsf{TCPIP}. \tag{7.9}$$

The nouns "Who" and "TCP/IP" were translated into the ontology concepts Person and TCPIP, whereas the transitive verb "invented" was translated into the ontology role invent. How role quantifiers ($\exists, \forall$) should be handled is discussed in section 7.5.1.

The question shown in (7.2) with its mapping depicted in table 7.2 could be translated into the following DL-concept description:

$$Q \equiv \mathsf{Thing} \sqcap \mathsf{Task} \sqcap \mathsf{Protocol}. \tag{7.10}$$

The nouns "What", "task", and "protocol" were translated into the ontology concepts Thing, Task, and $\mathsf{Protocol}$. The auxiliary verb "be", as well as the stop words "the", "of", and "a", were ignored. How this expression could be optimized is described in section 7.4.4.

The chunk "are the task of" could be processed as one token and interpreted as the ontology role taskOf. This would result in the following, more accurate logical form:

$$Q \equiv \mathsf{Thing} \sqcap \exists \mathsf{taskOf} \sqcap \mathsf{Protocol}. \tag{7.11}$$

Discussion

Although these three expressions may be sufficient for basic E-Librarian Services, especially if the user questions are short and simple questions, they may not provide a sufficiently accurate representation of the real world. As isolated words are not put into the context of a whole sentence, this strategy is more appropriate for a simple keyword search.

7.4.2 With Syntactic Analysis

The analysis of the structure of the sentence may improve its semantic interpretation. The idea is to consider the *syntax* of a sentence and to use linguistic relations between the words.

In fact, the syntactic structure of a sentence indicates the way how words in the sentence are related to each other, e.g., how the words are grouped together into phrases, which words modify which other words and which words are of central importance in the sentence (see section 4.4).

The syntactic analysis of a sentence is commonly performed by a *parser*. A list of parsers is given in appendix D.

For different implementations, we used *LoPar* because it is a lightweight, reliable, and easy-to-use parser, for Unix/Linux operating systems. The authors[3] also granted us permission to modify the dictionary so that we could adapt it to our needs. LoPar comprises parsing with a *head-lexicalized probabilistic context-free grammar* (HL-PCFG).

---

[3] Helmut Schmid and Sabine Schulte im Walde, Institut für Machinelle Sprachverarbeitung (IMS), University of Stuttgart.

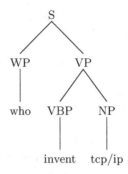

Fig. 7.6. Syntax tree of the sentence: "Who invented TCP/IP?"

Examples

Let us consider the question in (7.1), which would be parsed as shown in figure 7.6. The syntax of the sentence reveals that the verb "invent" and the noun "tcp/ip" are related, i.e., they are together on a branch of the syntax tree. Therefore, they must be connected in the logical form of the sentence as well. The verb "invent" is mapped to the ontology role invent. The way in which role quantifiers ($\exists, \forall$) should be handled is discussed in section 7.5.1. The noun "tcp/ip" is mapped to the ontology concept TCPIP and turns into the argument of the role. Finally, the most accurate interpretation would be:

$$Q \equiv \text{Person} \sqcap \exists \text{invent.TCPIP.} \tag{7.12}$$

A more complicated example is the semantic interpretation of the following question:

$$\textit{What are the tasks of a protocol?} \tag{7.13}$$

It would be parsed as shown in figure 7.7. To simplify the syntax tree, we suppose that determiners, auxiliary verbs, and pronouns are ignored. The simplified tree is depicted in figure 7.8.

The syntax of the sentence reveals that the nouns "task" and "protocol" are related, i.e., they are together on a branch of the syntax tree. As a result, they must be connected in the logical form as well. The problem with the simplified syntax tree is that there is no role for the DL-concept description since we ignore the auxiliary verb "be".

Several heuristics could be applied. First, the noun "task" could be mapped to the role taskOk instead of or in addition to the concept Task. The resulting logical form could then be:

$$Q \equiv \text{Thing} \sqcap \exists \text{taskOf.Protocol.} \tag{7.14}$$

Secondly, the chunk "the task of" could be mapped to the role taskOf, which would result in the same logical form as shown in (7.14).

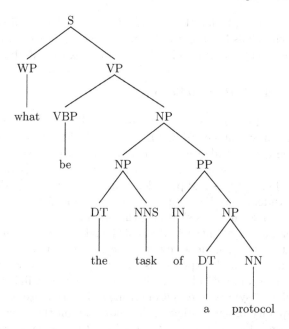

Fig. 7.7. Syntax tree of the sentence: "What are the tasks of a protocol?"

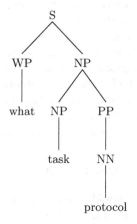

Fig. 7.8. Simplified syntax tree of the sentence: "What are the tasks of a protocol?"

Thirdly, the syntax of the sentence reveals that the noun "protocol" is the prepositional phrase (PP) of the noun phrase "task". This dependency can be expressed by using the concept Protocol as a filler of a role, e.g.,

$$Q \equiv \text{Thing} \sqcap \text{Task} \sqcap \exists \textbf{R}.\text{Protocol}. \tag{7.15}$$

Depending on the complexity of the NLP algorithm, the role **R** could remain a wildcard which stands for *any role*. Alternatively, a more accurate role could be identified by using heuristic rules like the ones explained above.

7.4.3 How much NLP is Sufficient?

NLP is a domain of ongoing research. There is still no reliable system that is able to translate any sentence from NL into a logical form. Therefore, NLP is always based on heuristic algorithms where compromises have to be accepted.

For instance, the approach presented in section 7.4.1 has been used and tested in several prototypes and provided sufficient efficiency [LM07]. In these experiments, students used E-Librarian Services and formulated short and precise questions like the ones shown in this section.

Furthermore, a strict syntax analysis of the NL questions is not possible if users are free to enter sentences any way they want. It is widely known that users rarely express search expressions in a very precise way and that they make spelling and grammatical errors. Therefore, a parser will have difficulties building meaningful syntax trees out of erroneously formulated user questions.

Also, the quality of the retrieval relies not only on the preciseness of the NLP, but also on other factors, like the quality of the semantic annotation of the document (see section 6.3).

Generally, all systems that interact with humans have some concepts about their users. If the system is dedicated to a certain group of users, e.g., students in a mathematics lesson, then predications about the nature of their questions can be made. The aim of an E-Librarian Service is to "understand" the meaning of the user questions and to deliver semantically relevant documents. Therefore, the level of NLP should be adapted to the expected kind and complexity of the users questions, to the quality of the semantic annotations, and to the expected granularity of the yielded results. Hence, *light parsing* like *partial parsing* or *shallow parsing*, is often a sufficient compromise.

7.4.4 Optimization and Normal Form

The semantic interpretation should generate a DL-concept description that is in a normal form, i.e., the *reduced concept description* (RCD). The RCD states that a concept description does not contain any redundant information. For the sake of illustration, let us suppose that we have the following terminology:

$$\text{Thing} \sqsubseteq \top$$
$$\text{Task} \sqsubseteq \text{Thing}$$
$$\text{Protocol} \sqsubseteq \text{Thing}$$

Consequentially, the following DL-concept description is not in RCD because it contains the same concept multiple times:

$$Q \equiv \text{Thing} \sqcap \text{Thing} \sqcap \exists\text{taskOf.}(\text{Thing} \sqcap \text{Protocol}). \tag{7.16}$$

The terminology defines that Protocol $\sqsubseteq$ Thing. Therefore, the concept Thing can be removed because it introduces no more specific information. The normalization of the above expression would result in:

$$Q \equiv \text{Thing} \sqcap \exists \text{taskOf}.\text{Protocol.} \qquad (7.17)$$

Definition 7.6 (reduced concept description). *Let $C \equiv A_1 \sqcap ... \sqcap A_n$ be a DL-concept description and $A_i, i \in [1..n]$ are clauses in C. C is reduced if either $n = 1$ or no clause in C subsumes the conjunction of the other clauses:*

$$\forall 1 \leq i \leq n : A - A_i \sqsubseteq A_i.$$

7.5 General Limitations and Constraints

NL is always informal; its translation into a formal language like DL is therefore never free of ambiguities. Knowledge about the expected user questions is useful to adapt the level of NLP, e.g., the type of parsing. In this section, we describe problems and provide suggestions on how to deal with special cases.

7.5.1 Role Quantifiers

The exact semantic interpretation of NL is very difficult when it comes to role quantifiers. Let us consider the following examples:

$$\text{What task must a protocol have?} \qquad (7.18)$$
$$\text{What task can a protocol have?} \qquad (7.19)$$

The question in (7.18) states a mandatory condition; every protocol must have a certain task and may have other tasks in addition to the obligatory task. This kind of formulation clearly indicates the use of the existential quantifier ($\exists$). The correct translation should be the following:

$$Q \equiv \text{Protocol} \sqcap \exists \text{hasTask}.\text{Task} \qquad (7.20)$$

The question in (7.19) states an optional feature; a protocol can have a certain task, but can also have no task at all. This kind of formulation indicates the use of the universal quantifierx ($\forall$). The correct translation should be the following:

$$Q \equiv \text{Protocol} \sqcap \forall \text{hasTask}.\text{Task} \qquad (7.21)$$

The correct interpretation of quantifiers is often ambiguous and subjective because DL quantifiers must not necessarily reflect the exact sense of the NL sentence. In more formal terms, the sentence expressed in (7.20) states that a protocol can have a task of the concept Task, but maybe other tasks from other concepts, e.g., $\exists \text{hasTask}.\text{Service}$. However, the sentence expressed in (7.21) states that a protocol can only have tasks from the concept Task. This subtle difference introduced by the semantics of quantifiers must not necessarily reflect the purpose of the user question.

It should be decided during the design of an E-Librarian Service whether different quantifiers really improve the expected retrieval or not. As the aim of an E-Librarian Service is to "understand" the sense of the question, the problem of interpreting quantifiers is in practice less important. If a less complex DL-language was used, like $\mathcal{EL}$, then the problem of quantifiers would be eliminated since such simple languages only offer limited use of quantifiers.

7.5.2 Conjunction and Disjunction

Conjunction

Generally, the word "and" stands for a conjunction and the word "or" for a disjunction. An example is the following:

$$\textit{Who invented TCP/IP and the WWW?} \tag{7.22}$$

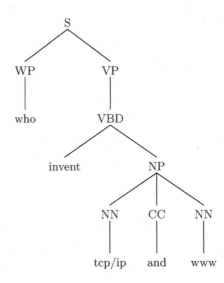

Fig. 7.9. Simplified syntax tree of the sentence: "Who invented TCP/IP and the WWW?"

The syntax of the sentence shown in figure 7.9 reveals that the words "TCP/IP" and "WWW" are connected by the conjunction (CC) "and". However, the concepts TCPIP and WWW in the resulting DL-concept description are conjuncted as well:

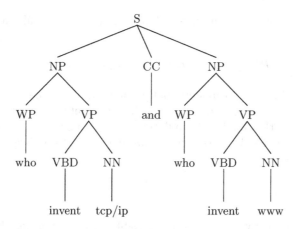

Fig. 7.10. Simplified syntax tree of the sentence: "Who invented TCP/IP and who invented the WWW?"

$$Q \equiv \mathsf{Person} \sqcap \exists \mathsf{invent}.(\mathsf{TCPIP} \sqcap \mathsf{WWW}). \tag{7.23}$$

This formula also expresses that TCP/IP and the WWW have been invented by the same person(s). If the user is looking for the inventor(s) of TCP/IP and the inventor(s) of the WWW, i.e., two different queries in one sentence, as depicted in figure 7.10, then the correct DL-concept description should be:

$$Q \equiv \mathsf{Person} \sqcap \exists \mathsf{invent}.\mathsf{TCPIP} \sqcap \exists \mathsf{invent}.\mathsf{WWW}. \tag{7.24}$$

Discussion about Role Quantifiers

As explained in the previous section, the use of role quantifiers is a major challenge in the semantic interpretation. Formally,

$$\exists R.(C \sqcap D) \not\equiv \exists R.C \sqcap \exists R.D,$$

therefore the formulas in (7.23) and (7.24) express different semantics.

If in formulation (7.23) the universal quantifier ($\forall$) was used instead of the existential quantifier ($\exists$), as shown in formulation (7.25), then this would have expressed that there might be someone who has only invented TCP/IP and the WWW, but nothing else. This is a very restricted formulation, which again shows that preference should be given to the existential quantifier over the universal quantifier.

$$Q \equiv \mathsf{Person} \sqcap \forall \mathsf{invent}.(\mathsf{TCPIP} \sqcap \mathsf{WWW}). \tag{7.25}$$

$$Q \equiv \mathsf{Person} \sqcap \forall \mathsf{invent}.\mathsf{TCPIP} \sqcap \forall \mathsf{invent}.\mathsf{WWW}. \tag{7.26}$$

The expression in (7.26) states that there might be one or different persons who have only invented TCP/IP and who have only invented WWW.

Although this seems to be an inconsistent formulation, formally it is logically sound because:

$$\forall R.(C \sqcap D) \equiv \forall R.C \sqcap \forall R.D \text{ iff } C \sqcap D \not\equiv \bot.$$

This query would yield documents that are individuals of the concepts TCPIP and WWW at the same time. Since such documents may not exist in the knowledge base, this kind of formulation remains risky and we recommend giving preference to the existential quantifier over the universal quantifier while dealing with roles.

Disjunction

As for disjunction, two scenarios are possible. Let us consider the following question for illustration:

$$\textit{Who invented TCP/IP or the WWW?} \tag{7.27}$$

If a more complex DL-language is used that provides the disjunction operator ($\sqcup$) like $\mathcal{ALC}$, $\mathcal{ALU}$, or $\mathcal{ALN}$, then the resulting DL-concept description could be:

$$Q \equiv \text{Person} \sqcap \exists\text{invent.}(\text{TCPIP} \sqcup \text{WWW}). \tag{7.28}$$

However, using such higher DL-languages raises the complexity of the reasoning algorithm and does not guarantee computation. Therefore, an alternative solution is to create two simpler concept descriptions and to merge the results of both queries, e.g.,

$$Q_1 \equiv \text{Person} \sqcap \exists\text{invent.TCPIP} \tag{7.29}$$

$$Q_2 \equiv \text{Person} \sqcap \exists\text{invent.WWW} \tag{7.30}$$

We suggest using the most simple DL-language that provides sufficient precision to represent the meaning of the user questions. In most of our implementations, we used the DL-language $\mathcal{EL}$ (see section 3.1.2). The same discussion about the use of quantifiers as made above is also valid for disjunction.

7.5.3 Negation

Negations can be expressed in different ways, but most often the adverb "not" is used. A simple way to deal with negations is to negate the concept or role it modifies. Let us consider the following sentence to illustrate the principle, even though such formulations are less realistic:

$$\textit{What is not a task of a protocol?} \tag{7.31}$$

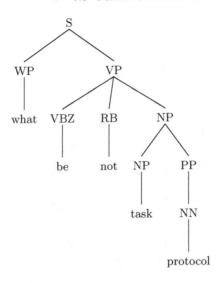

Fig. 7.11. Simplified syntax tree of the sentence: "What is not a task of a protocol?"

The syntax tree shown in figure 7.11 reveals that the negation (RB) "not" is over the complete noun phrase (NP) "a task of a protocol". The resulting DL-concept description could be:

$$Q \equiv \text{Thing} \sqcap \neg \exists \text{taskOf.Protocol} \tag{7.32}$$

The processing of negations in a sentence gets much more complicated when the negation is used in combination with a conjunction or disjunction, e.g.,

$$\textit{What is a task of a protocol and not of a router?} \tag{7.33}$$

Based on the syntax tree shown in figure 7.12, the resulting DL-concept description could be:

$$Q \equiv \text{Thing} \sqcap \exists \text{taskOf.}(\text{Protocol} \sqcap \neg \text{Router}). \tag{7.34}$$

7.5.4 Open-Ended and Closed-Ended Questions

Open-ended questions are a form of question which cannot be answered by using a simple "yes" or "no". They are generally preceded by a *w-word* like "what", "who", "where", or by the word "how". Here are some examples:

$$\textit{How does a protocol work?} \tag{7.35}$$

$$\textit{What are the tasks of a protocol?} \tag{7.36}$$

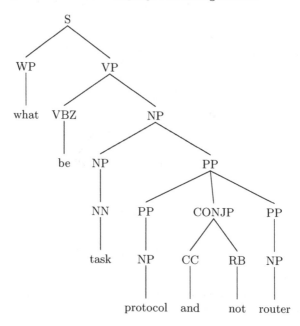

Fig. 7.12. Syntax tree of the sentence: "What is a task of a protocol and not of a router?"

Other formulations of open-ended questions are possible, though less frequent, e.g.,

$$\textit{Tell me about the tasks of a protocol!} \tag{7.37}$$

Since every example in this chapter has been an open-ended question, we will not discuss this topic any further.

Closed-ended questions are a form of question which can normally be answered by using a simple "yes" or "no". It is less frequent that users formulate closed-ended questions, e.g.,

$$\textit{Is error-handling a task of a protocol?} \tag{7.38}$$

To provide a complete illustration of the semantic interpretation of the question in (7.38), let us consider its syntax tree, as shown in figure 7.13, as well as the following terminology:

Thing ⊑ ⊤
Task ⊑ Thing
Protocol ⊑ Thing
Protocol ⊓ ∃hasTask.ErrorHandling ⊑ Task

After optimization, as described in section 7.4.4, the resulting logical form could be:

$$Q \equiv \text{ErrorHandling} \sqcap \exists \text{taskOf.Protocol}. \tag{7.39}$$

A straightforward solution to handle closed-ended questions is to process them as open-ended questions. The user can then decide whether the top-ranked answer(s) yielded by the E-Librarian Services should be considered as a "yes" or "no".

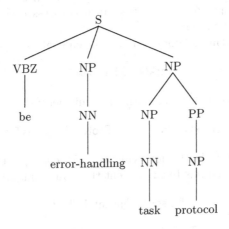

Fig. 7.13. Simplified syntax tree of the sentence "Is error-handling a task of a protocol?"

A more risky approach is to let the system decide whether the resulting documents represent a "yes" or a "no". "No" could be yielded if no matching document was found or if the top-ranked answer had a low accuracy or precision (see section 5.4).

7.5.5 Formulations

If users are free to enter NL sentences any way they want, different formulations to express the same thing are possible. For example, although the following two questions have different formulations and could be translated into different logical forms, their meaning is the same:

$$\text{NL:} \quad \textit{What are the tasks of a protocol?} \tag{7.40}$$
$$\text{DL:} \quad \text{Thing} \sqcap \exists \text{taskOf.Protocol} \tag{7.41}$$

$$\text{NL:} \quad \textit{What tasks does a protocol have?} \tag{7.42}$$
$$\text{DL:} \quad \text{Protocol} \sqcap \exists \text{hasTask.Task} \tag{7.43}$$

For a DL-system, both expressions are clearly different if not stated otherwise. As a human, we see that the second sentence is just another formulation of the first one and that the reading-direction of the sentence has changed. The key parts are the roles taskOf and hasTask.

The accurate translation of the verb into a DL-role is often challenging. DL allow to express equivalences (for simple DL-languages) and inverse functionalities between concepts and roles (for more complex DL-languages). In this way, different concept and role names can be processed as similar or inverse in order to reflect the reality more accurately.

To help the system to "understand" this equivalence, we can define:

$$taskOf \equiv hasTask^-$$

which makes both sentences semantically equivalent:

$$Thing \sqcap \exists taskOf.Protocol \equiv Protocol \sqcap \exists hasTask.Task.$$

A similar example is the following two DL-concept descriptions, which have different formulations but represent the same semantics:

$$Person \sqcap \exists invent.TCPIP \tag{7.44}$$

$$TCPIP \sqcap \exists inventedBy.Person \tag{7.45}$$

These two expressions are semantically equivalent if the equivalence between the roles invent and inventedBy is given, i.e.,

$$invent \equiv inventedBy^-$$

7.5.6 Others

Section 4.2.1 enumerates many difficulties which can result from free user formulations. It is not possible to provide a general framework for NLP that works for every situation. Hence, the most convenient solutions and algorithms to handle precise problems have to be designed for each system.

As this book is not dedicated to NLP, we will only list various problems that may be encountered while dealing with NL. The designer of an E-Librarian Service will have to decide if such formulations are allowed and how they should be processed.

- Punctuation marks and special characters (like hyphens and slashes), e.g., "TCP/IP", "error-handling", or "Dot.Five" can be considered as one token or as two different tokens.
- Abbreviations like "Lux." can be processed as a synonym for "Luxembourg", but can also represent different words (in this particular case, "Lux" could also stand for the unit of illuminance and luminous emittance).
- Quotation marks could be processed as separate sentence makers or tokens, e.g., "Who is 'the father' of TCP/IP?".

- Whitespace: different words can be processed as one token, e.g., proper names ("Did *Serge Linckels* invent TCP/IP?"), nouns ("Who invented the *hard drive?*"), or verbs ("Who *worked out* the architecture of TCP/IP?").
- Inter-clausal dependencies, e.g., "Is the person who invented TCP/IP also the person who invented Ada?".
- Hypotheses, e.g., "If we assume that Serge Linckels invented TCP/IP, would he also be considered to be the father of the Internet?".

7.6 Multiple-Language Feature

A very useful feature of the NLP module as presented in this chapter is its independency towards language. By simply changing the domain dictionary, e.g., a German dictionary instead of a French one and the parser, the complete E-Librarian Service can be used for a different language.

Role: invent
$s = $ demo:invent
$T_{English} = \{$invent, build, create$\}$
$T_{German} = \{$erfinden, bauen, erschaffen$\}$
$T_{French} = \{$inventer, construire, créer$\}$
$arg_1 = $ demo:Person
$arg_2 = $ demo:Thing

Fig. 7.14. Example of the role invent with multiple-language feature.

The domain dictionary entry for the role invent, as depicted in figure 7.14, shows support for English, German, and French. This does not mean that the same physical dictionary must handle different languages. The notion of domain dictionary, as used in an E-Librarian Service, is a mapping between a domain language, e.g., WordNet and an ontology (see section 7.3.2). In case of a multiple-language feature, several dictionaries are mapped to the same ontology.

The added value of this approach is that words from different languages will be mapped to the same ontology concepts and roles, e.g.,

$$\varphi(\text{"invent"}) = \varphi(\text{"erfinden"}) = \varphi(\text{"inventer"}) = \{\text{invent}\}$$

For a more complete example, let us consider the following user questions in English, German, and French respectively:

$$\textit{Who invented TCP/IP?} \qquad (7.46)$$

$$\textit{Wer hat TCP/IP erfunden?} \qquad (7.47)$$

$$Qui \ a \ inventé \ TCP/IP \ ? \tag{7.48}$$

As all three questions represent exactly the same meaning, but are formulated in different languages, their semantic interpretation will result in the same logical form:

$$Q \equiv \mathsf{Person} \sqcap \exists \mathsf{invent.TCPIP}. \tag{7.49}$$

The multiple-language feature was particulary useful in several experiments with an E-Librarian Service, where knowledge bases where used that contained documents in different languages. In this way, the same E-Librarian Service was able to process user questions in different languages whilst reasoning over the same knowledge base.

8

Designing the Multimedia Information Retrieval Module

The core component of an E-Librarian Service is the multimedia information retrieval (MIR) module that performs a *semantic search* over the knowledge base. Its task is to retrieve only semantically pertinent documents with respect to a given user query. Among all the documents in the knowledge base that have some common information with the user query, the MIR module is able to identify the most pertinent match(es), keeping in mind that the user in general expects an exhaustive answer while preferring a concise answer with only little or no information overload.

8.1 Overview of the MIR Module

An E-Librarian Service is an ontology-driven semantic search engine over a multimedia knowledge base. It is most efficient if the metadata is structured in an ontological way (see section 6). An overview of the MIR module is depicted in figure 8.1.

All computations are performed over the metadata and not over the content of the documents. Therefore, the performance in terms of response time is high and the search engine is independent of the media, i.e., documents like video, audio, or HTML.

8.1.1 Knowledge Base and metadata

To illustrate the principle of the MIR module, let us suppose that there are only 5 multimedia documents in the knowledge base: D_1 to D_5. The content of the documents deals with the following topics:

D_1: general information about computer networks and TCP/IP,

D_2: information about protocols and their tasks,

D_3: explanation that error-handling is a task of a protocol,

D_4: information about error handling,

D_5: explantation that Tim Berners-Lee (co-)invented the WWW.

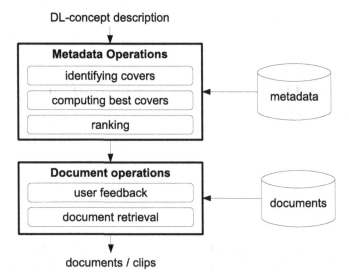

Fig. 8.1. Overview of the MIR module.

The E-Librarian Service performs its computations over structured meta-data which is expressed in Description Logics (DL). Hence, the metadata is a set of DL definitions with respect to a hierarchy of concepts (see chapter 3).

For the above example, a hierarchy of concepts is depicted in figure 8.2 and the corresponding semantic descriptions are shown in figure 8.3. We use the DL sub-language $\mathcal{EL}$, which has structural subsumption and allows conjunction ($\sqcap$), existential restriction ($\exists r.C$), and the top concept ($\top$).

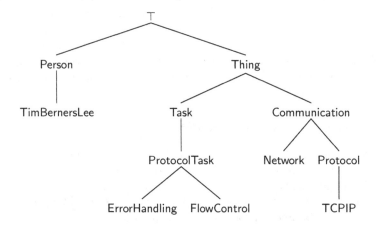

Fig. 8.2. Taxonomy about computer networks.

$$D_1 \equiv \text{Network} \sqcap \text{TCPIP}$$
$$D_2 \equiv \text{Protocol} \sqcap \exists\text{hasTask.ProtocolTask}$$
$$D_3 \equiv \text{Protocol} \sqcap \exists\text{hasTask.ErrorHandling}$$
$$D_4 \equiv \text{ErrorHandling}$$
$$D_5 \equiv \text{TimBernersLee} \sqcap \exists\text{hasInvented.WWW}$$

Fig. 8.3. Terminology of document definitions.

8.1.2 Retrieval Principle

By *retrieval* we refer to the idea of answering a user question by finding only the semantically most pertinent documents. Let us suppose that the user enters the question:

$$\textit{What are the tasks of TCP/IP?} \tag{8.1}$$

According to the NLP module described in chapter 7, this question could be translated into one of the following DL-concept descriptions:

$$Q \equiv \text{TCPIP} \sqcap \exists\text{hasTask.Thing} \tag{8.2}$$

$$Q \equiv \text{Thing} \sqcap \exists\text{taskOf.TCPIP} \tag{8.3}$$

The equivalence of both expressions has been explained in section 7.5.5 by defining the role hasTask as being the inverse of the role taskOf.

The principle of the retrieval algorithm is to identify which document descriptions (D_1 to D_5) share some information with the query. To find the best matching documents among all candidate-documents, we refer to the notion of *semantic distance* (or semantic relatedness); the smaller the semantic distance between the query and the candidate-document, the more pertinent the document is for the user. The search results can eventually be ranked by their semantic distance to the query.

Many alternative approaches exist that are also based on the computation of some semantic relatedness. We refer the interested reader to the following resources: [MBR01, dFE06, BWH05, BH06, KEW01].

The strategy used by an E-Librarian Service is based on the *concept covering problem*. It will be described in section 8.1.3. First, it is an efficient solution for finding semantically pertinent documents by inferring over the knowledge base. Secondly, it is based on simple DL sub-languages with structural subsumption which provide sufficient expressiveness. Thirdly, the retrieval algorithm always returns a correct and optimal answer.

8.1.3 The Concept Covering Problem

Two document descriptions can have a common part of information; their intersection or overlapping part. If there is no intersection, then the document descriptions are disjoint. If the intersection is equal to both document descriptions, then the documents are semantically equivalent. The three situations are depicted in figure 8.4.

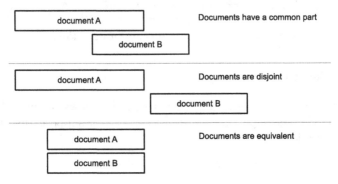

Fig. 8.4. Document descriptions can have common parts.

Original Concept Covering Problem

The original concept covering problem defines a *cover* as being the conjunction of some document descriptions that share some information with a query (see section 3.4.2). Based on the illustration given in figure 8.5, valid covers are, e.g.,

$$cover(\text{query}) = \text{document A} \sqcap \text{document B}$$
$$cover(\text{query}) = \text{document D}$$
$$cover(\text{query}) = \text{document E}$$
$$cover(\text{query}) = \text{document C} \sqcap \text{document B}$$

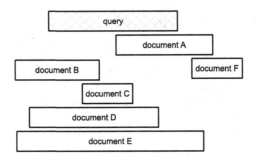

Fig. 8.5. query and possible covers.

In fact, all document descriptions except document F and all conjunctions of document descriptions are covers. A *best cover* is the conjunction of document descriptions that covers the query completely. According to the examples in figure 8.5, best covers are:

$$cover(\mathsf{query}) = \mathsf{document\ A} \sqcap \mathsf{document\ B} \sqcap \mathsf{document\ C}$$
$$cover(\mathsf{query}) = \mathsf{document\ A} \sqcap \mathsf{document\ D}$$
$$cover(\mathsf{query}) = \mathsf{document\ E}$$

Modified Concept Covering Problem

Although the principle of the original concept covering problem is pertinent for an E-Librarian Service, the user might not be satisfied if the delivered answer to a precise question is a concatenation of different, possibly not related, documents. First, there is no transition between the different documents. Secondly, we risk that there is way too much information in the delivered answer, because the original algorithm adds all necessary and (partially) matching documents to the answer until the query is covered completely.

Users prefer few, but precise answers, even if these answers are not exhaustive, rather than a set of different concatenated documents. They are looking for one, "the best", answer, and tend to reformulate their query to reduce the number of results.

The modified concept covering problem defines a *cover* (candidate-document) as being a document description that shares some information with the query. *best covers* are the document descriptions which have the largest common part and do not deliver too much supplementary information.

Finally, an E-Librarian Service always delivers an answer, even if there is no exhaustive one. By quantifying the missing and supplementary information, the system is able to compute and to visualize the pertinence of the yielded document(s).

8.2 Identifying Covers

Based on a user query, the first task of the MIR module is to identify candidate-documents. These documents have some information in common with the query. Such documents are called *covers* (see section 8.1). For example, the following table shows the part of information that each document description in figure 8.3 has in common with the query in (8.3).

document	cover
D_1	TCPIP
D_2	Protocol $\sqcap$ $\exists$hasTask.Thing
D_3	Protocol $\sqcap$ $\exists$hasTask.Thing
D_4	Thing
D_5	$\top$

It is important to remember that the computation of the cover takes into account implicit knowledge from the document descriptions, i.e., inferred information from the terminology. To illustrate this mechanism, we expand the concept description of document D_4 and the query Q with respect to the hierarchy of concepts depicted in figure 8.2, as explained in section 3.2.1. After expansion we get:

$$D_4 \equiv \textbf{Thing} \sqcap \textsf{Task} \sqcap \textsf{ProtocolTask} \sqcap \textsf{ErrorHandling},$$

$$Q \equiv \textbf{Thing} \sqcap \textsf{Communication} \sqcap \textsf{Protocol} \sqcap \textsf{TCPIP} \sqcap \exists \textsf{hasTask}.\textsf{Thing}.$$

Hence, the only parts which both concept descriptions have in common is the concept Thing. It thus seems evident that document D_4 is only poorly related to the query.

The above table provides the information that document D_5 has nothing in common with the query. Therefore, it will no longer be considered for the current query. All other documents are covers.

The next task of the MIR module will be to determine which covers are the best covers, i.e., which documents are semantically the most related to the query. This task will be described in section 8.3.

Definition 8.1 (cover). *Let $\mathcal{L}$ be a Description Logic with structural subsumption, $\mathcal{T}$ be a $\mathcal{L}$-terminology and $C_{\mathcal{T}} = \{C_i \not\equiv \bot, i \in [1, n]\}$ the set of concept descriptions occurring in $\mathcal{T}$. Then $C_j \in C_{\mathcal{T}}$ is a cover of a $\mathcal{L}$-concept description $Q \not\equiv \bot$, if $Q - lcs_{\mathcal{T}}(Q, C_j) \not\equiv Q$, where the operator $-$ represents the semantic difference and lcs is the least common subsumer.*

Both non-standard reasoning services, i.e., the *semantic difference* and the *least common subsumer* (lcs), are explained in chapter 3. By using the *lcs* in the computation of the cover, implicit data from the terminology are made explicit, as shown in the above example.

8.3 Computing the Best Covers

The *cover* is what each document has in common with the query. The *best cover* can be defined based on the information that is required by the query, but not delivered by the document and the information that the document delivers additionally.

8.3.1 Miss and Rest

The data that is required by the query, but not delivered by the document, is called *miss* (see definition 8.2). The data that the document delivers additionally, but which was not required by the query, is called *rest*. The smaller both are, the closer the document is to the query. Figure 8.6 depicts the principle of cover, miss, and rest.

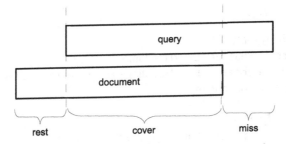

Fig. 8.6. Graphical illustration of *cover*, *miss*, and *rest*.

Definition 8.2 (miss and rest). *Let Q and C be be two $\mathcal{L}$-concept descriptions, then:*

- *the miss of Q with respect to C, denoted as $miss(Q,C)$ is defined as:*

$$miss(Q,C) = Q - lcs_T(Q,C),$$

- *the rest of Q with respect to C, denoted as $rest(Q,C)$ is defined as:*

$$rest(Q,C) = C - lcs_T(Q,C).$$

To illustrate the computation of the miss and rest, we consider the terminology given in figure 8.3 and the query in (8.3).

For document D_1:

$$
\begin{aligned}
rest &= D_1 - lcs(Q, D_1) \\
&= \text{Network} \sqcap \text{TCPIP} - lcs(Q, D_1) \\
&= \text{Network} \sqcap \text{TCPIP} - \text{Thing} \\
rest &= \text{Network} \sqcap \text{TCPIP}
\end{aligned}
$$

$$
\begin{aligned}
miss &= Q - lcs(Q, D_1) \\
&= \text{TCPIP} \sqcap \exists \text{hasTask.Thing} - lcs(Q, D_1) \\
&= \text{TCPIP} \sqcap \exists \text{hasTask.Thing} - \text{TCPIP} \\
miss &= \exists \text{hasTask.Thing}
\end{aligned}
$$

For document D_2:

$$
\begin{aligned}
rest &= D_2 - lcs(Q, D_2) \\
&= \text{Protocol} \sqcap \exists \text{hasTask.ProtocolTask} - lcs(Q, D_2) \\
&= \text{Protocol} \sqcap \exists \text{hasTask.ProtocolTask} - (\text{Protocol} \sqcap \exists \text{hasTask.Thing}) \\
rest &= \exists \text{hasTask.ProtocolTask}
\end{aligned}
$$

$$
\begin{aligned}
miss &= Q - lcs(Q, D_2) \\
&= \text{TCPIP} \sqcap \exists \text{hasTask.Thing} - lcs(Q, D_2) \\
&= \text{TCPIP} \sqcap \exists \text{hasTask.Thing} - (\text{Protocol} \sqcap \exists \text{hasTask.Thing}) \\
miss &= \text{TCPIP}
\end{aligned}
$$

For document D_3:

$$rest = D_3 - lcs(Q, D_3)$$
$$= \text{Protocol} \sqcap \exists \text{hasTask.ErrorHandling} - lcs(Q, D_3)$$
$$= \text{Protocol} \sqcap \exists \text{hasTask.ErrorHandling} - (\text{Protocol} \sqcap \exists \text{hasTask.Thing})$$
$$rest = \exists \text{hasTask.ErrorHandling}$$

$$miss = Q - lcs(Q, D_3)$$
$$= \text{TCPIP} \sqcap \exists \text{hasTask.Thing} - lcs(Q, D_3)$$
$$= \text{TCPIP} \sqcap \exists \text{hasTask.Thing} - (\text{Protocol} \sqcap \exists \text{hasTask.Thing})$$
$$miss = \text{TCPIP}$$

For document D_4:

$$rest = D_4 - lcs(Q, D_4)$$
$$= \text{ErrorHandling} - lcs(Q, D_4)$$
$$= \text{ErrorHandling} - \text{Thing}$$
$$rest = \text{ErrorHandling}$$

$$miss = Q - lcs(Q, D_4)$$
$$= \text{TCPIP} \sqcap \exists \text{hasTask.Thing} - lcs(Q, D_4)$$
$$= \text{TCPIP} \sqcap \exists \text{hasTask.Thing} - \text{Thing}$$
$$miss = \text{TCPIP} \sqcap \exists \text{hasTask.Thing}$$

The semantic distance between the query and a document is computed by quantifying the miss and rest. The smaller both are, the closer the document is to the query.

8.3.2 Size of a Concept Description

The miss and rest are DL concept descriptions. To quantify them in terms of integers, we need to measure the size of a concept description (see definition 8.3).

Definition 8.3 (size of a concept description). *The size of a concept description, denoted as $|\cdot|$, is inductively defined by:*

- $|\bot| = |\top| = 0,$
- $|A| = |\neg A| = 1,$
- $|\exists R.C| = |\forall R.C| = 2 + |C|,$
- $|C \sqcap D| = |C \sqcup D| = |C| + |D|,$
- $|\neg C| = |C|.$

where C and D are two concept descriptions, A is an atomic concept, and R is a role.

We defined the size of an atomic concept as 1 and the size of a role as 2. We have chosen these values based on our experiences. Any other values could be used as well, as long as they remain unchanged for all computations. Let us consider the following concept description to illustrate the computation of its size:

$$Q \equiv \mathsf{TCPIP} \sqcap \exists \mathsf{hasTask.Thing}$$

which has the following size:

$$
\begin{aligned}
|\mathsf{TCPIP}| &= 1 \\
|\exists \mathsf{hasTask}| &= 2 \\
\underline{|\mathsf{Thing}|} &= 1 \\
|Q| &= 4
\end{aligned}
$$

Discussion

The definition of the size of a DL-concept description ignores structural information, i.e., the number of arcs in the hierarchy of concepts that have to be traversed to arrive at the given concept. Thus, the size of the following two concept descriptions would be identical:

$$|A_1 \sqcap \exists R.(A_2 \sqcap \exists S.A_3)| = 7$$

$$|A_1 \sqcap A_2 \sqcap A_3 \sqcap \exists R \sqcap \exists S| = 7$$

One could argue that in the first concept description, the atomic concept A_3 should be semantically less important because it is nested deeper in the structure than concept A_1. A solution could be to introduce a negative score that takes into account structural information.

The definition given in (8.3) was sufficient in all our E-Librarian Services. Firstly, it is a fair measure for any concept description. Secondly, and most importantly, user questions are generally simple formulations which rarely result in a complex logical form. An example of a question which would result in a more complex concept description is:

What mother has a daughter who is a doctor and whose child is a professor?

Mother $\sqcap \exists \mathsf{hasChild.}(\mathsf{Mother} \sqcap \exists \mathsf{isDoctor} \sqcap \exists \mathsf{hasChild.}\exists \mathsf{isProfessor})$

For all computations of the size of a concept description in the remaining part of this book, we use the formulae provided in definition (8.3).

8.3.3 Best Covers

The best cover can be assumed as being the cover with the smallest miss and rest (see definition 8.4). We give preference to a minimized miss. In fact, the

E-Librarian Service aims to give an exhaustive answer in the first place, i.e., to yield an answer that covers the user query as much as possible, even if there is more information in the answer than required. The rest is considered only in second place in order to rank the results that have the same miss.

To illustrate the principle of best cover, let us consider table 8.1. It shows the size of the miss and rest as computed in section 8.3.1. Documents D_2 and D_3 have the smallest miss, whereas document D_4 has the smallest rest.

	rest		miss	
D_1	$|\text{Network} \sqcap \text{TCPIP}| = 2$		$|\exists \text{taskOf.Thing}| = 3$	
D_2	$|\exists \text{hasTask.ProtocolTask}| = 3$		$|\text{TCPIP}| = 1$	
D_3	$|\exists \text{hasTask.ErrorHandling}| = 3$		$|\text{TCPIP}| = 1$	
D_4	$|\text{ErrorHandling}| = 1$		$|\text{TCPIP} \sqcap \exists \text{hasTask.Thing}| = 4$	

Table 8.1. Size of miss and rest for each document.

The documents D_2 and D_3 are best covers because they have the smallest miss. Although the information they deliver is not complete, i.e., there is still a miss ≥ 0, it is the best information that the system can provide.

It is interesting to notice that the concept TCPIP does not appear in one of the best covers, although it appears in the query and in D_1. This shows that the best cover is not computed on a statistical evaluation of keywords, but that it is in fact the result of the logical inference.

Definition 8.4 (best cover). *Let Q and C be two $\mathcal{L}$-concept descriptions. A cover C is called a best cover with respect to Q using a terminology $\mathcal{T}$ iff:*

- *C is a cover with respect to Q using $\mathcal{T}$ and*
- *there does not exist any cover C' of Q using $\mathcal{T}$ such that*

$$(|miss(Q, C')|, |rest(Q, C')|) < (|miss(Q, C)|, |rest(Q, C)|)$$

where $<$ stands for the lexicographic order.

By choosing a lexicographical order we give preference to a minimized miss. For example, for (miss,rest), the couple (1,2) is smaller than (2,1) because the first couple has a smaller miss than the second one.

8.4 Ranking

By considering the miss and rest, the MIR module is able to quantify the quality of the yielded result(s), i.e., to measure the semantic distance between the user query and the candidate-documents. This measure is used to rank the documents in the answer set.

The list of ranked documents can be commented according their pertinence.

- If a document with $miss = 0$ and $rest = 0$ is found, then the system "knows" that this is a perfect answer with no information missing and no information overload.
- A document with $miss = 0$ and $rest > 0$ will provide a full answer to the user question, but it delivers some information that was not asked.
- All other results where $miss, rest > 0$ provide an incomplete answer.
- Results where $miss > threshold$ can be marked as not pertinent because their semantic distance is too far from the actual query.

The pertinence of a document from the answer set can be visualized by the E-Librarian Service, so that the user sees the quality of the delivered results at one glance. The user can then either reformulate the question or read the provided documents. For the example shown in table 8.1, the list of ranked results would be:

rank	pertinence	document	comment
1.	best covers	D_2 and D_3	but uncomplete and information overload
2.	cover	D_1	but uncomplete and information overload
3.	cover	D_4	but uncomplete and information overload

Document D_5 would not be yielded because it is not a cover and therefore would deliver no answer to the query.

Example of a Running System

The E-Librarian Service depicted in figure 8.7 was developed to provide a semantic search engine over the online archive of university lectures at the Hasso-Plattner-Institute[1]. The figure shows the retrieved results for the question:

$$What \ is \ an \ IP\text{-}address \ composed \ of? \qquad (8.4)$$

Best covers are emphasized in a different color. The pertinence of the delivered documents is indicated by stars. The E-Librarian Service also finds the exact part of the answer inside a video document and presents the position of that sequence in a different color.

8.5 Algorithm for the Retrieval Problem

An algorithm to compute best covers is shown in figure 8.8. As input, a query Q is expected which was translated into a DL-concept description (see chapter 7) and a terminology $\mathcal{T}$, i.e., a set of semantic descriptions of documents (see chapter 6). The output is the set E of best covers with respect to Q.

The algorithm works as follows: $C_\mathcal{T}$ is the set of semantic descriptions of the documents in the knowledge base. Each document is tested if it is a cover

---

[1] http://www.tele-task.de/

Fig. 8.7. Presentation of the search results for the question: "What is an IP-address composed of?"

(line 4). If so, then it will only be maintained, if either the size of its miss is smaller than (line 5) or equal to (line 8) the smallest miss found up to now. In the first case, the current document replaces all the former best cover candidates (lines 6 + 7). In the second case, the current document is added to the best cover candidates found up to now (line 9).

8.6 User Feedback

In this section, we will briefly present some ideas on how to improve the quality of an E-Librarian Service by using the user's intellectual capabilities. These are: direct user feedback, collaborative tagging and social networks, and diversification of user feedback.

Require: a query $Q \not\equiv \bot$, a set of concept descriptions $C_T = \{C_i \not\equiv \bot, i \in [1, n]\}$
Ensure: a set of best covers $E = \{C_j \in C_T, j \in [0..n]\}$
1: $E \leftarrow \emptyset$
2: $MinMiss \leftarrow +\infty$
3: **for** each $C_i \in C_T$ **do**
4:     **if** $Q - lcs(Q, C_i) \not\equiv Q$ **then**
5:       **if** $|Miss(Q, C_i)| < MinMiss$ **then**
6:         $E \leftarrow C_i$
7:         $MinMiss \leftarrow |Miss(Q, C_i)|$
8:       **else if** $|Miss(Q, C_i)| = MinMiss$ **then**
9:         $E \leftarrow E \cup C_i$
10:       **end if**
11:     **end if**
12: **end for**

Fig. 8.8. Algorithm to compute best covers.

8.6.1 Direct User Feedback

Direct user feedback can be achieved in different forms. The most simple way is to let the user determine whether a given result set of documents really is appropriate according to his question or not. An E-Librarian Service could keep track of user feedback and channel that data into the rank computation of the document result set.

An E-Librarian Service faces the problem to provide both an *objective answer*, as well as a feedback-driven and therefore more or less *subjective answer*. Therefore, it could display both the (objective) best covers and the (subjective) feedback-based results. Thus, the user would have the possibility to see objectively computed results and the results according to the opinion of other users.

8.6.2 Collaborative Tagging and Social Networks

User-generated keywords (*tags*) might be an additional source for the semantic annotation of documents in a knowledge base. A user might provide additional, otherwise unavailable semantic annotation. In this regard, *collaborative tagging* has known an ever-increasing popularity, which is demonstrated by the growing number of prominent tagging and annotation sites such as Del.icio.us[2], Flickr[3], or Bibsonomy[4].

An additional source of information could be provided by the *social networking* information of the tagging service. Based on this networking informa-

---

[2] http://www.del.icio.us/
[3] http;//www.flickr.com/
[4] http://http://www.bibsonomy.org/

tion a similarity measure for documents could be determined. Users who have tagged the same documents with the same or similar keywords, concepts, or roles could be considered to have similar or common interests. By retrieving documents with similar tags, similar documents could be determined.

8.6.3 Diversification of User Feedback

Different users asking the same question might expect different answers. This is due to the fact that different users prefer different levels of complexity, of difficulty, and of elaborateness. Moreover, different users come from different backgrounds, have different motivations, and thus have a different context. The user could be given the means to specify whether he prefers complex and precise documents, or if a short overview about the requested topic is sufficient.

An E-Librarian Service could keep track of the user's actions; statistics could then be gathered about document usage. If a user has already accessed and used a given document, this information could be used to customize the computation of the best cover with respect to the previous knowledge of the user.

9

Implementation

This book is dedicated to the principles of designing an E-Librarian Service and its underlaying technologies. Part 1 of this book was dedicated to the principles and necessary technologies to build such a system. In part 2, we explained how to design an E-Librarian Service. In this chapter, we provide details and recommendations on how to implement an E-Librarian Service and focus on the architecture and several details about the development of such a system.

9.1 Architecture

An E-Librarian Service is an interactive and distributed system. The principle is to keep the required technology on the user's side as simple as possible, so that no special installation or configuration is necessary. As a result of the influences of Semantic Web technologies and theories (see chapter 2), an E-Librarian Service is developed around a straight-forward layer architecture.

The architecture is composed of four main layers (see figure 9.1): the Knowledge Layer, the Inference Layer, the Communication Layer, and the Presentation Layer. This modularized approach is helpful for possible extensions and the evolution of an E-Librarian Service; modules can be exchanged by new ones without affecting the complete system.

9.1.1 Knowledge Layer

The Knowledge Layer is the set of data sources which are accessed by the Inference Layer for reasoning over the knowledge. The data sources are: the domain dictionary, the domain ontology, and a terminology. The domain language is used for the natural language processing (NLP), as explained in chapter 7. The domain ontology gives the necessary information about the

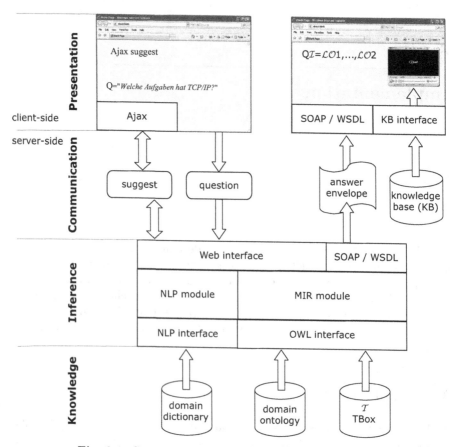

Fig. 9.1. General architecture of our E-Librarian Service.

complete domain (see chapter 6). The terminology delivers the semantic description of the documents in the knowledge base (see chapter 8). Both, the ontology and the terminology, are encoded as OWL-files.

9.1.2 Inference Layer

The Inference Layer is the most important one because it implements the *semantic search engine*; all the reasoning is done at this level. It is composed of the NLP module (see chapter 7), the MIR module (see chapter 8), and the different interface sub-layers (see sections 9.2.2 and 9.2.3).

In a simplified view, the Inference Layer works as follows: it receives a question in natural language (NL) from the upper layer, translates it into a logical form, computes the best answer, and returns the references (URIs) of the pertinent documents to the upper layer. In addition, the inference engine is able to "understand" if it has the correct or at least a good answer, and is able to explain to the user the quality of the delivered answer, i.e., the *semantic distance* between the entered question and the yielded documents.

The communication with the upper Presentation Layer is based on two requirements. First, the answer to the user question must be available for the user in a very short time. This excludes sending the whole resulting document(s) to the user. Instead, only the URI and some metadata about the document(s) are transmitted. It is up to the client application how this data will be presented to the user.

Secondly, the Inference Layer must be transparent to the user, independently of the fact whether the inference engine runs as a process (service) on the user's local machine or if it is accessed distantly as a Web service. Hence, the answer of the Inference Layer must be encoded in a platform and system independent way. For example, in a software oriented architecture, the list of pertinent documents is encapsulated into a *SOAP envelope* (see section 9.2.3) that can be unfolded on the client side.

9.1.3 Communication Layer

The Communication Layer allows a transparent communication between the client application (Presentation Layer) and the semantic search engine (Inference Layer). It should not be important if these two layers are on the same machine or not. Furthermore, the communication must be error-free, transparent, and hardware independent.

Some E-Librarian Services employ a service-oriented architecture (SOA) to offer a standardized access to the inference engine via a *SOAP/WSDL interface* (see section 9.2.3). This allows developers to create their own client application that communicates with the inference engine and is fully compatible with the current evolution of the Semantic Web.

In other E-Librarian Services, the Communication Layer was based on a low level *socket communication*. Using sockets has three advantages: it uses the popular protocol TCP/IP, it offers an error-free transmission, and components for most development environments are widely available.

9.1.4 Presentation Layer

The Presentation Layer represents the interface between the user and the machine. It gets a question from the user and transmits it to the semantic search engine via the Communication Layer. In return, it displays the search result(s) and allows the user to read the yielded document(s). In some E-Librarian Services, the Presentation Layer is implemented as a Web page (see section 9.2.2).

We would like to mention different possible qualities that can be implemented in order to improve the Presentation Layer. First, an interface that automatically adapts to the user, i.e., a simple interface for children and a more expressive interface for experts. Beside the pure layout problems, XML transformation (XSLT) could be used to filter too complicated documents from the answering set. This is helpful because different users might prefer different levels of complexity, of difficulty and of elaborateness. Other interesting approaches are for instance scalable metadata [LTV03] or meta-modeling teachware [SF99].

9.2 Development Details

In this section, we will describe three technical details about the implementation of an E-Librarian Service: the processing of OWL and Description Logics (DL) in Java, a special "auto-suggest" feature for the input of NL, and the Web service interface.

9.2.1 Processing OWL and DL in Java

In all our implementations, the semantic search engine was developed in Java in order to guarantee platform independency. The *Jena API*[1] [CDD+04] is most commonly used in Java to process RDF/OWL. However, Jena has very limited reasoning capacities and does not have non-standard inference services, like the least common subsumer or the concept covering problem on which relies the MIR module (see chapter 8).

There are different external reasoners, like Fact++[2] [BVL03], RacerPro[3] [HM01], KAON2[4], and Pellet[5] [SP04]. A list of current DL reasoners can be found here: [Gro10]. However, they support only standard interference services, like subsumption and satisfiability.

In the remaining part of this section, we present a simple and optimized datastructure for representing DL-concept descriptions and algorithms for reasoning over the data (see figure 9.2). In this model, a DL-concept description is composed of generic terms (DLTerm). Each term is identified by its URI. For example, the concept TCPIP has the following URI:

http://www.linckels.lu/demo/elements/1.0#TCPIP

The classes DLConcept (lines 9 – 13) and DLrole (lines 15 – 20) inherit from the generic DLTerm (lines 1 – 7) and represent DL-concepts and DL-roles respectively. DLRole is special because a role can have a list of arguments (line 16), which again are of the type DLTerm. Finally, a DL-concept description, implemented in the class DLDescription (starting at line 28), is among a set of operations, simply a list of terms (line 29).

---

[1] http://jena.sourceforge.net/
[2] http://owl.man.ac.uk/factplusplus/
[3] http://www.racer-systems.com/
[4] http://kaon2.semanticweb.org/
[5] http://pellet.owldl.com/

```
 1: class DLTerm {
 2: // Generic class(concept or role)
 3:    String uri;
 4:    DLTerm(String uri) {
 5:       this.uri = uri;
 6:    } // constructor DLTerm
 7: } // DLTerm
 8:
 9: class DLConcept extends DLTerm {
// A DL concept
10:    DLConcept(String uri) {
11:       super(uri);
12:    } // constructor DLConcept
13: } // DLConcept
14:
15: class DLRole extends DLTerm {
// A DL role
16:    DLDescription args;
17:    DLRole(String uri) {
18:       super(uri);
19:       args = new DLDescription();
20:    } // constructor DLRole
21:
22: void add(DLTerm t) {
23:       // adds a term to the arguments
24:       args.add(t);
25:    } // add
26: } // DLRole
27:
28: class DLDescription {
// A DL-concept description
29:    ArrayList terms;
30:    DLDescription() {
31:       super();
32:       terms = new ArrayList();
33:    } // constructor DLDescription
       ...
}
```

Fig. 9.2. Datastructure for representing DL-concepts, -roles and -concept descriptions.

This simple datastructure is based on Java *ArrayList*. This special type of container is a generic and resizable array of objects, which comes with highly optimized operations. In a benchmark test, a set of 120 questions was processed in approximately 10 seconds whilst the data was represented with the above structure. When the Jena datastructure and algorithms were used, the same test took approximatively 5 minutes.

For illustration, we describe two operations over our datastructure: quantification of the size of a DL-concept description and the computation of the least common subsumer.

Quantification of the Size of a DL-Concept Description

The method quantify() for the class DLDescription quantifies the size of a DL-concept description according to definition 8.3 in section 8.3. It is invoked with the command C.quantify(), where C is an instance of the class DLDescription. The result of the method is a positive integer. The code is shown in figure 9.3.

It works as follows: a standard iterator is used to browse through the list of terms in the DL-concept description (line 3). Each term adds at least the value 1 to the size n of the DL-concept description (line 5). If the term is a role, then n is incremented by the size of the arguments of the role, which are recursively computed (line 7).

```
 1:  int quantify() {
 2:     int n = 0;
 3:     for (Iterator i = terms.iterator(); i.hasNext();) {
 4:        DLTerm t = (DLTerm) i.next();
 5:        n++;
 6:        if (t instanceof DLRole)
 7:           n = n + ((DLRole) t).args.quantify();
 8:     } // for i
 9:     return n;
10:  } // quantify
```

Fig. 9.3. Method that quantifies the size of a DL-concept description.

Computation of the Least Common Subsumer

The method lcs() for the class DLDescription computes the least common subsumer (lcs) of two DL-concept descriptions according to definition 3.2 in section 3.4.2. It is invoked with the command D.lcs(C), where C and D are instances of the class DLDescription. The result of the method is a DL-concept description representing the lcs of C and D. The code is shown in figure 9.4.

It works as follows: a standard iterator is used to browse through the terms of the DL-concept description D (line 5). Each term is tested if it also exists in the DL-concept description C (lines 9 and 10). The method **contains** returns *true* if a given term is found in the referenced DL-concept description. If the term exists in C, then it is added to the resulting list of the lcs if it is a concept (line 26 – 27). If the referenced term is a role (line 13), then both roles must be compared. There are three possibilities: the role name and the role arguments match, then the complete role is added to the resulting lcs-concept description (lines 17 – 19), only the role names match, then only the role name is added to the resulting lcs-concept description (lines 20 – 22) or there is no match at all, then the role is ignored.

```
 1: DLDescription lcs(DLDescription C) {
 2:   DLDescription res = new DLDescription();
 3:
 4:   // Browse through description of this object
 5:   for (Iterator i = terms.iterator(); i.hasNext();) {
 6:     DLTerm t = (DLTerm) i.next();
 7:
 8:     // check if this term is in C
 9:     DLTerm u = C.contains(t);
10:     if (u != null) {
11:
12:        // t is a role
13:        if (t instanceof DLRole) {
14:          DLRole r = (DLRole) t;
15:
16:          // check if the role's arguments match
17:          if (r.args.equal(((DLRole) u).args))
18:            // yes -> add the complete role
19:            res.add(r);
20:          else
21:            // no -> add only name of role (new role)
22:            res.add(new DLRole(r.uri));
23:        } // if role
24:
25:        // t is a concept
26:        else
27:          res.add(t);
28:      } // if not contained
29:   } // while
30:
31:   return res;
32: } // lcs
```

Fig. 9.4. Method that computes the lcs.

9.2.2 Client Front-End with Ajax Autocompleter

The basic task of the Presentation Layer is to allow people to express their questions in NL and to read/watch the resulting document(s). The graphical user interface (GUI) should be as simple and ergonomic as possible.

A feature of an E-Librarian Service can be to assist the user to compose a NL question, e.g., by providing a "suggestion textfield" (or autocompleter). When the user strikes a key, then this information is immediately transmitted to the Web server, which returns a list of words that start with this character. The user can select one word from that suggestion-list or can continue to type the word. For each additional character, the suggestion list is refreshed.

This feature has at least three advantages. First, it helps the user to quickly assemble the words to form a complete sentence. Secondly, the risk of spelling errors in the sentence is reduced. Thirdly, only words from the domain dictionary of the system are used, which will result in a very reliable semantic interpretation of the user's questions.

Of course, the user can use words that are not known by the system. In that case, these words are logged and can be added later to the domain dictionary by the administrator.

```
1:  <html> <head> ...
2:    function initAutocompleter() {
3:      new MyAutocompleter("autocomplete",
                            "autocomplete_choices",
                            suggestions );
4:    } // initAutocompleter
      ...
5:  </head>
6:  <body onLoad="initAutocompleter()">
      ...
7:      <input type="text" id="autocomplete"
              name="txtQuestion" size="50" />
8:      <div id="autocomplete_choices"
            class="autocomplete" />
      ...
9:  </body> </html>
```

Fig. 9.5. Textfield with Ajax suggestion list.

The code of the suggestion textfield is shown in figure 9.5. The *autocompleter* is initialized when the Web site is loaded (line 6). This means that an instance of the autocompleter-class `MyAutocompleter` is created and a reference to the textfield `autocomplete` and the layer `autocomplete_choices` is made (line 3). The variable `suggestions` is a JavaScript-array that contains the list of all possible words, i.e., a local copy of the domain dictionary. The suggestion textfield is a standard HTML-textfield that references the Ajax-class `autocomplete` (line 8). The HTML-layer `autocomplete_choices` is the window that contains the list of suggested words (line 9). It is automatically refreshed each time the user strikes a key.

9.2.3 The SOAP Web Service Interface

In some E-Librarian Services, the communication between the Presentation Layer and the Inference Layer is done by low-level socket communication. Other E-Librarian Services are implemented as Web services to offer a more universal communication interface with a standardized SOAP interface. This has the advantage that every developer can build his own application that uses our semantic search engine, while the transportation of the NL question and the set of yielded documents remains transparent.

In some E-Librarian Services, the open source *Apache Axis*[6] is used as Web service framework. It consists of a Java and a C++ implementation of the SOAP server, as well as various utilities and APIs for generating and deploying Web service applications. When a Web service is exposed using Axis, it will automatically generate a *WSDL* file when accessing the Web service URL with ?WSDL added to it. The *Web Services Description Language* (WSDL) is an XML-based language that provides a model for describing Web services. Version 2.0 is a W3C recommendation[7]. The WSDL defines services as collections of network endpoints or ports. Finally, the complete E-Librarian Service can easily be assembled in an .aar-file—which is nothing else than a Java archive (jar)—and deployed as a Web service. It is accessible via the HTTP interface, e.g., `http://theHostName:8080/axis2/services/demo?wsdl`.

SOAP is a protocol for exchanging XML-based messages over computer networks, normally using HTTP(S). SOAP originally stood for *Simple Object Access Protocol* and lately also *Service-Oriented Architecture Protocol*, but is now simply SOAP. The original acronym was considered to be misleading and was therefore dropped with Version 1.2 of the standard, which became a W3C Recommendation[8] in June 2003.

There are several different types of messaging patterns in SOAP, but the most common one by far is the *Remote Procedure Call* (RPC) pattern, in which one network node (the client) sends a request message to another node (the server) and the server immediately sends a response message to the client. SOAP makes use of an Internet application layer protocol as a transport protocol. Both SMTP and HTTP are valid application layer protocols used as transport for SOAP, but HTTP has gained wider acceptance as it works well with today's Internet infrastructure. XML was chosen as the standard message format because of its widespread use by major corporations and open

---

[6] `http://ws.apache.org/axis/`
[7] `http://www.w3.org/TR/wsdl`
[8] `http://www.w3.org/TR/soap/`

source development efforts. Additionally, a wide variety of freely available tools significantly ease the transition to a SOAP-based implementation.

```
  . . .
 1: // read question from HTML-form
 2: $question = $_POST['txtQuestion'];
 3:
 4: // submit query to Web service via SOAP
 5: require_once 'SOAP/Client.php';
 6: $wsdl_url = 'http://localhost:8080/demo?wsdl';
 7: $WSDL = new SOAP_WSDL($wsdl_url);
 8: $client = $WSDL->getProxy();
 9: $params = array("$question");
10:   $answer = $client->search($params);
  . . .
```

Fig. 9.6. SOAP communication with the semantic search engine.

Figure 9.6 illustrates how an E-Librarian Service can be accessed via SOAP. The example shows some PHP-code that reads a user question (line 2). The connection with the Web service is established (lines 5 – 8) and the remote procedure **search()** is called with the user question as argument (lines 9 – 10). The remote procedure returns the answer encoded as string. In our prototype, this answer-string contains the URIs of the different documents, as well as ranking information, i.e., the semantic distance.

Part III

Applications

10

Best practices

In this chapter, we present three best practices of E-Librarian Services that have been tested in real life scenarios.

- *CHESt*, an E-Librarian Service which covers the main events in computer history.
- *MatES*, which was specifically designed for a pedagogical project as a "virtual mathematics teacher".
- *The Lecture Butler*, which allows students to find information inside videos of recorded university lectures.

10.1 Computer History Expert System (CHESt)

10.1.1 Description

The E-Librarian Service *CHESt* stands for *Computer History expert system* and was developed in 2004. The tool has a knowledge base with 300 multimedia clips in German language that cover the main events in computer history. The clips were recorded with *tele-TASK*[1] at the University of Trier.

The MIR module was implemented in Java. The user can access the search engine via a Windows application developed in *Delphi*, as depicted in figure 10.1. CHESt is based on a complete distributed architecture; the semantic search engine, the knowledge base, and the user application can be on different machines. The communication is transparent and is done using socket connections. *Pellet*[2] [SP04] was used as external reasoner.

CHESt exists in different configurations. It turned out that the following two were the most suitable.

---

[1] http://www.tele-task.de/
[2] http://clarkparsia.com/pellet/

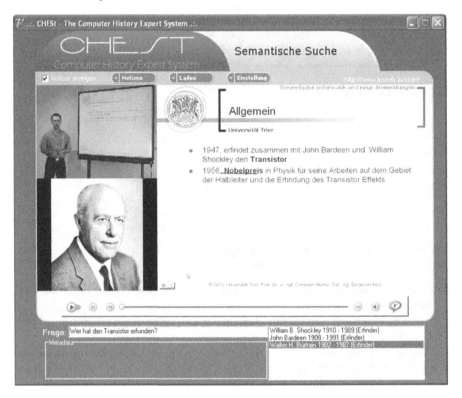

Fig. 10.1. CHESt with the question: "Who invented the transistor?"

- The search engine was installed on a server in a wired network, and each user had a local copy of the client application. The knowledge base was accessed via a streaming server. This configuration is the most secure one, because nobody has direct access to the clips and to the search engine. The quality and performance of the network play a key role in the reliability of this configuration because the streaming of the videos can produce congestion problems.
- All components are on the user's machine. CHESt fits on one CD-ROM, including the knowledge base, the search engine, and the client application. This configuration has the highest reliability and performance and generates no network traffic. Its disadvantage is that everyone has direct access to the application and the knowledge base and could make unauthorized copies.

A useful feature of CHESt is that the user can take notes. While watching a clip, the user can at any time pause the playback and add a note at that time position. Next time the clip is played, this note is displayed at the same time-mark.

10.1.2 Experiment

In an experiment, test users were asked to try two search engines which both had the same graphical user interface (GUI). The first one performed a keyword-based search and the second one used an E-Librarian Service. The users were asked to provide feedback on the three main characteristics of the tools: the number of results, the pertinence of the results, and the satisfaction with the possibility to enter complete question(s) in natural language (NL) instead of keywords.

Description of the Experiment

None of the subjects had further domain knowledge about computer history. One half of each group started with the keyword-based search, the other half with the semantic search. After 20 minutes, the users were asked their opinion about the tested tools on a number of questions, and they then repeated the experiment in a second trial, this time with the other version of the search engine.

At the beginning of each session, the users were informed that two search engines allowing to search for information from the domain of computer history would be presented to them. They were told that the aim of the session would not be their successful answering of the frame questions, but rather their personal evaluation of the efficiency and their general appreciation of each search engine.

They were also briefed that the GUI would be the same for both versions and that no questions would have the GUI as target. The users were informed that their main job would consist in judging whether the search results yielded by the respective search engine would match their queries and whether they had really found the information they had been looking for.

Outcomes and Lessons Learned

Few users seemed to plan their search. In fact, the majority of all users started to enter the questions in exactly the same way as they were presented or they entered keywords that were used in the formulated questions. The interactive nature of CHESt supported the users' belief that there was no need to plan ahead because the progression of a search would be largely determined by what they saw on the screen. Most actions were new queries and relatively few users refined their searches by specialization, generalization, or reformulation.

A clear difference in strategy depends on the experience of the participants. As demonstrated in our experiment, novices typically start with very general queries and gradually narrow down the search, adding and changing their queries. This leads to the outcome that users need guidance in how to formulate effective queries, especially if they are not experts in the focused domain.

One interesting realization is that a majority of users turned out to use only keywords to formulate queries, independently of the used search engine. Several users commented that they were simply more at ease with a keyword-based search.

An interesting observation was that when a search did not return the expected result, users tended to re-enter a previous query where they were sure to get a result. Users often return to "landmarks" where they have received good answers.

We observed that a lot of users judged the pertinence of the answers of the system and the quality of the search engine by the number of results that were returned. Most users appreciated a short list of results. If a search returned too many results, most users quickly browsed through the list, selected one document randomly from the answer set or tried another query. Some users launched different queries without consulting any answer, only to reduce the number of results.

Asked how they chose a clip among the list of results, the majority of the users were not able to give a precise explanation. Most of them selected one clip randomly, started to watch it and decided relatively quickly if that answer was pertinent.

Users make quick decisions about whether or not a document is relevant. Users have clear expectations about the requested search result. A result was often not accepted if that clip only contained some pieces of the expected answer. Users wanted one document to include all the information they needed.

Finally, 22% of the users preferred entering complete questions instead of keywords, 69% preferred entering complete questions instead of keywords only if this yielded better results, and 8% disliked this option.

10.2 Mathematics Expert System (MatES)

10.2.1 Description

The E-Librarian Service *MatES* stands for *Mathematics Expert System* (see figure 10.2). It was specifically designed to be used for a pedagogical experiment in a secondary school in Luxembourg in 2006.

The knowledge base covers the topic of fractions in mathematics. Most of the 115 clips were recorded by pupils at the Lycée Technique d'Esch/Alzette (LTE). The clips were recorded in French because it is the language used to teach mathematics in Luxembourg; the search engine therefore used a French dictionary.

Similarly to the E-Librarian Service CHESt (see section 10.1), the semantic search engine was implemented in Java. The client application was developed in Delphi. Since MatES was created for students to be used at home or in a classroom, it was mainly used in the following two configurations:

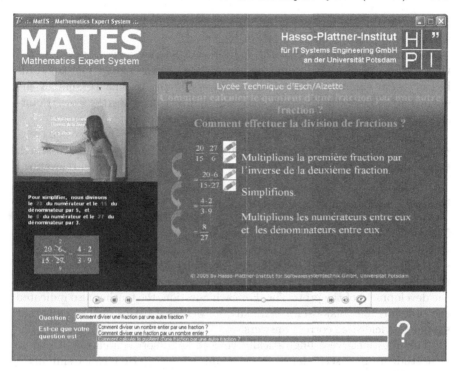

Fig. 10.2. MatES with the question: "How to divide one fraction by another fraction?"

- A "Home Edition", where the knowledge base, the semantic search engine, and the user application were on one DVD. No configuration or installation procedure was necessary to use MatES. This configuration was used in the mentioned experiment because it was the most reliable and the simplest to use.
- A "Classroom Edition", where the semantic search engine and the knowledge base were installed on an application server in a wired network and every student had a local copy of the client application. This configuration was more secure than the first one, because nobody had direct access to the clips and the search engine.

In both cases, no streaming server was required and the user had high-speed access to the clips. The response time of the system to process a question and to deliver its answer was between 3 and 5 seconds.

10.2.2 Benchmark Test

The quality of the E-Librarian Service was evaluated with a benchmark test. Benchmarks are designed to mimic a particular type of workload on a component or system. The test was performed on a standard Windows XP computer with a 1.4 GHz CPU and 512 MB of RAM.

The results obtained with the E-Librarian Service were then compared with the results of a traditional keyword-based search engine. The keyword-based search engine usually works by browsing the textual content of the documents. The textual content was generated by converting the PowerPoint-slides used to create the video recordings into pure text.

A document is considered as being a potential answer, if at least one (relevant) keyword from the user's query can be found. The keyword-based search engine does not consider stop words, i.e., words with no semantic relevance.

Knowledge Base and Set of Questions

The knowledge base about fractions in mathematics is composed of 115 clips, which cover the important subjects on fractions that are taught in secondary schools in Luxembourg. A testing set of 229 different questions about fractions in mathematics was created by a mathematics teacher, who was not involved in the development of the prototype. For each question, the teacher also indicated the best possible answer-clip manually, as well as a list of further clips that should be yielded as correct answers.

The questions were linguistically correct and short sentences, like those that students in a secondary school would ask, e.g., "How can I simplify a fraction?", "What are fractions good for?", "Who invented the fractions?", or "What is the sum of $\frac{2}{3}$ and $\frac{7}{4}$?" For the latter, the semantic interpretation would result in the following expression:

$$\text{Fraction} \sqcap \exists \text{hasOperation.Sum.} \qquad (10.1)$$

For this example, one clip, which explains how to add two fractions, would be retrieved. This would be the best clip that could be found in the knowledge base keeping in mind that our E-Librarian Service returns clips that explain the answer to the student's question without providing the answer itself, e.g., it does not compute the sum of the two fractions. This also means that questions like "How can I add two fractions?" or "What is $\frac{11}{0.5}$ plus $\frac{5}{5}$?" would yield the same clip.

On the contrary, the keyword search engine would yield all clips in which keywords like "sum" can be found, e.g., a clip that explains how to represent a complex fraction in terms of additions, or a clip that explains how to describe situations with simple fractions.

Benchmark Results

The processing time of all questions was about 2 to 4 seconds. The results of the benchmark test were the following. First, the semantic search engine

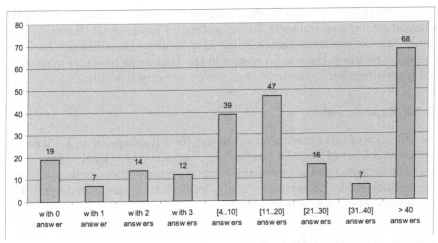

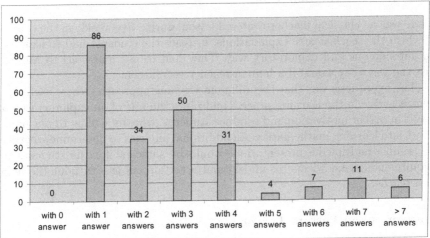

Fig. 10.3. Number of results yielded by a (1) keyword-based and by an (2) E-Librarian Service with a set of 229 questions.

answered 97% of the questions (223 out of 229) correctly, whereas the keyword-based search engine yielded a correct answer (i.e., a pertinent clip) only for 70% of the questions (161 out of 229).

Secondly, the semantic search engine yielded for 86 questions (37%) just one answer, i.e., the semantically best matching (figure 10.3). For 74% of the questions (170 out of 229), the semantic search engine yielded just a few results (one, two, or three answers), whereas the keyword-based search yielded for only 14% of the questions less than 4 answers; for 138 out of 229 question, it yielded more than 10 answers.

Thirdly, the E-Librarian Service always returned at least one result. This is important because students dislike getting no result at all. However, this feature has the weakness that it is not able to make the difference between a question to which there is no answer in the knowledge base and a question that has no relation to the topic, e.g., "Who invented penicillin?"

10.2.3 Experiment

The objective of this experiment was to test the advantages of an E-Librarian Service as a kind of "virtual teacher" in a normal educational environment and to investigate to what extent this alters students' school results positively. The prototype MatES was specifically developed for this experiment. The outcomes were published in [LDM06].

Description of the Experiment

There was no classical teacher-centered lesson, during five weeks, in the course of which the teacher gave explanations; instead, the students had to learn in an autonomous and exploratory way. They had to ask questions to MatES just the way they would if a human teacher was present.

The hypothesis was that this different training approach (where each student is active in the learning process and plays the role of an explorer) would result in higher motivation and produce students, who are willing to put more effort into learning mathematics. An additional aim was to determine whether the simple multimedia presentations would be sufficient for the students to acquire enough knowledge to understand a certain subject without the help of a teacher.

Outcomes and Lessons Learned

The data from the tests show that the students had better results when they used MatES. However, it cannot be proven if these improvements were really the direct consequence of the use of MatES. It is a fact that working with MatES was more motivating for the students, which in turn had a positive influence on the students' learning and understanding. Therefore, MatES indirectly contributed to improving the students' school results.

When asked if they think that they learned better with MatES compared to classical teaching, i.e., on geometry, 54.5% of the students were sure they did, 27.3% of the students answered somehow yes, 13.6% of the students said no, and 4.6% of the students did not know. The large majority of the students thought that their results in school could be improved with MatES.

The students were also asked if they enjoyed working with MatES. 50% of the students said "yes", 40.9% of the students said "yes, a lot", and 9.1% of the students said "somehow yes". None of the students disliked working with MatES.

One important question was about the constraint to enter complete questions. No student said that this was awkward. 31.8% of the students answered that they accepted entering a complete question but that they did not like it, and 68.2% of the students answered that this was no problem at all.

Students quickly acquired the specific vocabulary about fractions. If an unknown expression was used in a clip, they could then simply ask MatES to explain it.

Did the explanations from MatES help the students to get a better understanding of the explanations from classical sources (e.g., books, notes on the blackboard or verbal explanations from the teacher)? Nearly all students stated that they found the right information using MatES and most of the students stated that they learned better with MatES. Here are some explanations:

- The quality of the E-Librarian Service was a crucial factor of the success of MatES. It is well known that students generally dislike getting multiple results; they do not even consider all of them [FDD+99]. Students have clear expectations about the requested search result. The semantic search engine helped the students to find a good answer quickly; in other words, they did not have to wait for the teacher to answer their question.
- The use of new technologies is in general motivating for students. A similar conclusion is drawn from [PBR06], where students use tablet PCs, and from [HPM05], where a game-like tool was used to stimulate learning by making unpopular subjects fun.
- The student is active in his learning process. Everyone is constantly actively engaged and is able to build his knowledge through his own action. The lessons can be perceived as a kind of adventure where the student plays the role of an explorer who discovers new information.
- In traditional courses, more advanced or skilled students generally perform better, which is frustrating for less advanced learners. The use of an E-Librarian Service allows each student to progress at his own pace and according to his own capacities; no one is embarrassed.

10.3 The Lecture Butler's E-Librarian Service

10.3.1 Description

The E-Librarian Service "Lecture Buttler" was developed in the context of the Web University project at the HPI[3], which aims at exploring novel Internet and IT technologies in order to enhance university teaching and research (see figure 10.4). The objective is to create a tool for the learner that assists the student in his learning process. The Lecture Butler is a collection of different utilities, e.g., for creating a personalized lecture flow [KLM07], for mobile

---

[3] http://www.hpi.uni-potsdam.de/meinel/forschung/web_university.html

learning [WLM07], or for the semantic indexing of lecture videos [RM06]. Another feature of the Lecture Butler is an E-Librarian Service as a semantic search engine over the video archive.

The development of the Lecture Butler's E-Librarian Service started in summer 2006. It focused on a lecture series from the online tele-TASK archive about Internetworking[4] ("Internet- und WWW-Technologien") by professor Christoph Meinel, which is a set of 37 units with a total of over 50 hours of recorded lectures. The lecture units were split into smaller clips, with the idea that users generally ask short and precise questions and expect short and precise answers. They prefer short clips with a length of some minutes to complete lectures of 90 minutes.

The "Lecture Butler's E-Librarain Service" is a Web application. It offers a standardized Web interface to respect a service-oriented architecture (SOA). This allows every developer to write his own application that uses the search capabilities of this E-Librarian Service. This feature is described in more detail in section 9.2.3.

An ontology about networking in computer science was designed for this E-Librarian Service. It is illustrated in figure 6.4. Currently, the ontology contains 608 concepts and 26 roles.

10.3.2 Benchmark Tests

This benchmark test was made to verify the quality of the used E-Librarian Service over a knowledge base where all the documents are semantically very related. However, it was a more complex task for the tested search engines to find the best clip(s).

We chose the lecture about Internetworking from the online tele-TASK archive as knowledge base and created a set of 123 user questions about the topic Internetworking. We tried to work out typical student questions, e.g., "How does a datapacket find its way through a network?", "What is a switch good for?", "Do internet protocols guarantee an error-free communication?" or "What is an IP address composed of?" The latter example would be translated into the following expression:

$$IPAddress \sqcap \exists isComposedOf. \qquad (10.2)$$

Evaluation Constraints

For this evaluation, we call an answer from the E-Librarian Service a *perfect hit* if it covers the query completely, i.e., where $miss = rest = 0$ (see chapter 8). We call an answer a *sufficient hit* if it covers the query completely, but the answer contains more information than necessary, i.e., where $miss = 0$ and $rest > 0$.

---

[4] http://www.tele-task.de/page42_model_series599.html

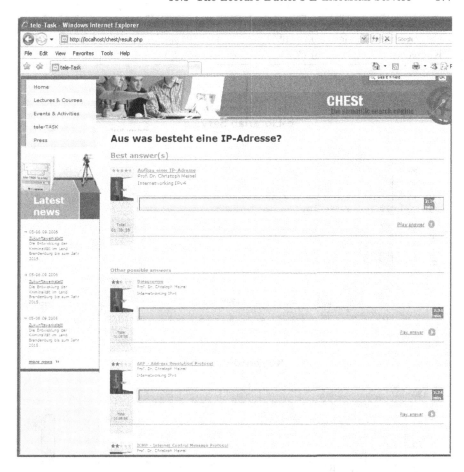

Fig. 10.4. Presentation of the search results with the Lecture Butler's E-Librarian Service for the question: "What is an IP-address composed of?"

For the evaluation, we only considered the *best covers* with minimal *miss* while ignoring the second choices. This means that if the E-Librarian Service did not deliver an exhaustive answer $(miss = 0)$ as best cover, but only as a second choice, we considered the answer to be wrong.

Outcomes and Results

The processing time of the first question was about 200 ms, while for the rest it was less than 10 ms. The outcomes of the benchmark test are the following.

First, the E-Librarian Service scored better than the keyword-based search regarding the pertinence of the results. In most cases the E-Librarian Service yielded the correct answer as depicted in the following table:

search engine	perfect hits	sufficient hits	total queries
E-Librarian Service	93 (76%)	112 (91%)	123 (100%)
Keyword search	9 (7%)	103 (84%)	123 (100%)

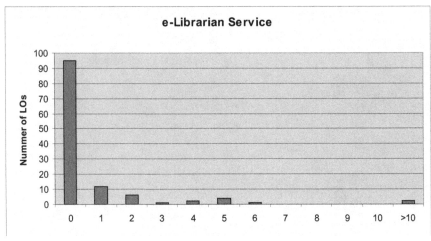

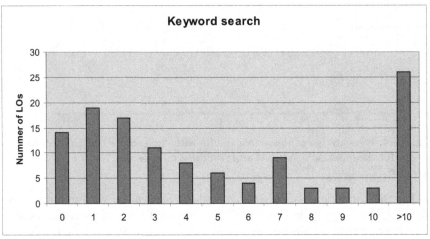

Fig. 10.5. Number of supplementary clips yielded with the optimal answer.

Secondly, the precision of E-Librarian Service is confirmed by the fact that on average less than 0.7 clips are returned in addition to the perfect answer (compared to 6 clips for the keyword-based search). Figure 10.5 shows the number of supplementary clips being supplied in addition to the expected answer. This important outcome demonstrates that the E-Librarian Service usually achieves the correct answer with no additional information (93 out of

123) and in a few cases one (12 out of 123) or two (6 out of 123) supplementary clips. The keyword-based search engine in general returns a lot more secondary clips.

This result is important evidence for the quality of the E-Librarian Service; the user asks a precise question and expects few, but concise answers. However, the keyword-based search leaves the user with the awkward task of filtering the pertinent answers out of the noise.

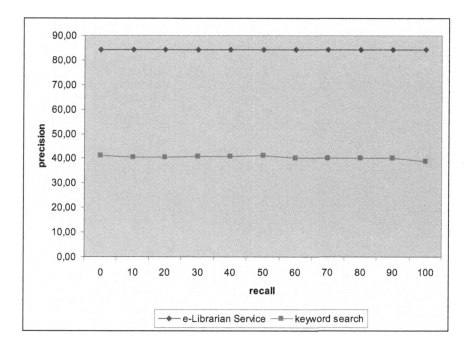

Fig. 10.6. Average precision at 11 standard recall levels.

Thirdly, figure 10.6 shows the average precision curve for both retrieving algorithms: the E-Librarian Service and the keyword-based search. Generally, the precision curves fall with increasing recall. This is not the case in our evaluation due to the fact that for each question in the test set, there are only few relevant documents to be retrieved (in average 1.29 relevant answers per question). For an average recall-level, the precision of the algorithm is 84.41%, compared to 40.42% for the keyword-based search.

These numbers confirm the previous outcome that the E-Librarian Service has a very high precision concerning the pertinence of the yielded answers; its average precision is more than twice as much as the precision achieved with the keyword-based search.

Part IV

Appendix

A

XML Schema Primitive Datatypes

`xs:anyURI`	URI (Uniform Resource Identifier)
`xs:base64Binary`	Binary content coded as "base64"
`xs:boolean`	Boolean (true or false)
`xs:byte`	Signed value of 8 bits
`xs:date`	Gregorian calendar date
`xs:dateTime`	Instant of time (Gregorian calendar)
`xs:decimal`	Decimal numbers
`xs:double`	IEEE 64-bit floating-point
`xs:duration`	Time durations
`xs:ENTITIES`	Whitespace-separated list of unparsed entity references
`xs:ENTITY`	Reference to an unparsed entity
`xs:float`	IEEE 32-bit floating-point
`xs:gDay`	Recurring period of time: monthly day
`xs:gMonth`	Recurring period of time: yearly month
`xs:gMonthDay`	Recurring period of time: yearly day
`xs:gYear`	Period of one year
`xs:gYearMonth`	Period of one month
`xs:hexBinary`	Binary contents coded in hexadecimal
`xs:ID`	Definition of unique identifiers
`xs:IDREF`	Definition of references to unique identifiers
`xs:IDREFS`	Definition of lists of references to unique identifiers
`xs:int`	32-bit signed integers
`xs:integer`	Signed integers of arbitrary length
`xs:language`	RFC 1766 language codes
`xs:long`	64-bit signed integers
`xs:Name`	XML 1.O name
`xs:NCName`	Unqualified names

`xs:negativeInteger`	Strictly negative integers of arbitrary length
`xs:NMTOKEN`	XML 1.0 name token (NMTOKEN)
`xs:NMTOKENS`	List of XML 1.0 name tokens (NMTOKEN)
`xs:nonNegativeInteger`	Integers of arbitrary length positive or equal to zero
`xs:nonPositiveInteger`	Integers of arbitrary length negative or equal to zero
`xs:normalizedString`	Whitespace-replaced strings
`xs:NOTATION`	Emulation of the XML 1.0 feature
`xs:positiveInteger`	Strictly positive integers of arbitrary length
`xs:QName`	Namespaces in XML-qualified names
`xs:short`	32-bit signed integers
`xs:string`	Any string
`xs:time`	Point in time recurring each day
`xs:token`	Whitespace-replaced and collapsed strings
`xs:unsignedByte`	Unsigned value of 8 bits
`xs:unsignedInt`	Unsigned integer of 32 bits
`xs:unsignedLong`	Unsigned integer of 64 bits
`xs:unsignedShort`	Unsigned integer of 16 bits

B

Reasoning Algorithms

As pointed out in section 3.4, approaches for solving inference problems are usually based on satisfiability and subsumption. There are two types of algorithms for solving subsumption: *structural subsumption* and *tableau algorithms*.

B.1 Overview

Structural subsumption algorithms compare the syntactic structure of concept descriptions. While they are usually very efficient, they are only complete for rather simple languages with little expressivity. In particular, DLs with (full) negation and disjunction cannot be handled by structural subsumption algorithms. For such languages, so-called tableau-based algorithms have turned out to be very useful.

Tableau algorithms are usually employed for DLs that allow full negation. Testing subsumption is reduced to deciding satisfiability of concepts. As stated in section 3.4.1, subsumption can always be reduced to satisfiability for DLs with full negation. For instance, $C \sqsubseteq D$ iff $C \sqcap \neg D \equiv \bot$.

B.2 Structural Subsumption

Algorithms for structural subsumption usually proceed in two phases. First, the DL-concept descriptions to be tested for subsumption are in a *normal form*, e.g., reduced concept description. Secondly, the syntactic structure of the normal forms is compared.

For example, a DL-concept description is in $\mathcal{EL}$-normal form if it has the following form:

$$A_1 \sqcap ... \sqcap A_n \sqcap \exists R_1.C_1 \sqcap \exists R_m.C_m,$$

Here, $A_1 \sqcap ... \sqcap A_n$ are distinct concept names, $R_1 \sqcap ... \sqcap R_m$ are distinct role names, and $C_1 \sqcap ... \sqcap C_m$ are DL-concept descriptions in normal form. In other words, a concept description is in its $\mathcal{EL}$-normal form if it does not contain any redundant information.

Definition B.1 (structural subsumption). *Let C, D be two concept descriptions in their normal form, i.e.,*

$$C \equiv A_1 \sqcap \ldots \sqcap A_m \sqcap \exists R_1.C_1 \sqcap \exists R_n.C_n,$$

$$D \equiv B_1 \sqcap \ldots \sqcap B_k \sqcap \exists S_1.D_1 \sqcap \exists S_l.D_l,$$

then $C \sqsubseteq D$ iff the following two conditions hold:

- $\forall 1 \le i \le k, \exists 1 \le j \le m : B_i = Aj,$
- $\forall 1 \le i \le l, \exists 1 \le j \le n : S_i = R_j \text{ and } C_j \sqsubseteq D_i.$

B.2.1 Example 1

For the sake of illustration, let us consider the following concept descriptions, where $C \sqsubseteq D$ with structural subsumption holds:

$$C \equiv \mathsf{Human} \sqcap \mathsf{Female} \sqcap \mathsf{Woman} \sqcap \exists \mathsf{hasChild.Woman},$$

$$D \equiv \mathsf{Human} \sqcap \mathsf{Woman} \sqcap \exists \mathsf{hasChild.Human}.$$

B.2.2 Example 2

A second example where structural subsumption fails is the following:

$$A \sqcap \neg A \sqsubseteq^? B \sqcap \neg B,$$

which results in testing:

$$(A \sqsubseteq^? B \vee A \sqsubseteq^? \neg B) \wedge (\neg A \sqsubseteq^? B \vee \neg A \sqsubseteq^? \neg B).$$

The result would be "no"; none of the four subsumption tests holds. However, $A \sqcap \neg A \equiv \bot$ and $B \sqcap \neg B \equiv \bot$. Therefore, $A \sqcap \neg A \sqsubseteq B \sqcap \neg B$ results in testing if $\bot \sqsubseteq \bot$ holds, which is the case.

C

Brown Tag Set

Tag	Definition
.	sentence closer (. ; ? *)
(	left paren
)	right paren
*	not, n't
−	dash
,	comma
:	colon
ABL	pre-qualifier (quite, rather)
ABN	pre-quantifier (half, all)
ABX	pre-quantifier (both)
AP	post-determiner (many, several, next)
AT	article (a, the, no)
BE	be
BED	were
BEDZ	was
BEG	being
BEM	am
BEN	been
BER	are, art
BEZ	is
CC	coordinating conjunction (and, or)
CD	cardinal numeral (one, two, 2, etc.)
CS	subordinating conjunction (if, although)
DO	do
DOD	did
DOZ	does

DT	singular determiner/quantifier (this, that)
DTI	singular or plural determiner/quantifier (some, any)
DTS	plural determiner (these, those)
DTX	determiner/double conjunction (either)
EX	existential there
FW	foreign word (hyphenated before regular tag)
HV	have
HVD	had (past tense)
HVG	having
HVN	had (past participle)
IN	preposition
JJ	adjective
JJR	comparative adjective
JJS	semantically superlative adjective (chief, top)
JJT	morphologically superlative adjective (biggest)
MD	modal auxiliary (can, should, will)
NC	cited word (hyphenated after regular tag)
NN	singular or mass noun
NN$	possessive singular noun
NNS	plural noun
NNS$	possessive plural noun
NP	proper noun or part of name phrase
NP$	possessive proper noun
NPS	plural proper noun
NPS$	possessive plural proper noun
NR	adverbial noun (home, today, west)
OD	ordinal numeral (first, 2nd)
PN	nominal pronoun (everybody, nothing)
PN$	possessive nominal pronoun
PP$	possessive personal pronoun (my, our)
PP$$	second (nominal) possessive pronoun (mine, ours)
PPL	singular reflexive/intensive personal pronoun (myself)
PPLS	plural reflexive/intensive personal pronoun (ourselves)
PPO	objective personal pronoun (me, him, it, them)
PPS	3rd. singular nominative pronoun (he, she, it, one)
PPSS	other nominative personal pronoun (I, we, they, you)
QL	qualifier (very, fairly)
QLP	post-qualifier (enough, indeed)
RB	adverb
RBR	comparative adverb

RBT	superlative adverb
RN	nominal adverb (here, then, indoors)
RP	adverb/particle (about, off, up)
TO	infinitive marker to
UH	interjection, exclamation
VB	verb, base form
VBD	verb, past tense
VBG	verb, present participle/gerund
VBN	verb, past participle
VBZ	verb, 3rd. singular present
WDT	wh- determiner (what, which)
WP$	possessive wh- pronoun (whose)
WPO	objective wh- pronoun (whom, which, that)
WPS	nominative wh- pronoun (who, which, that)
WQL	wh- qualifier (how)
WRB	wh- adverb (how, where, when)

D

Part-of-Speech Taggers and Parsers

D.1 POS Taggers

- Alembic Workbench
  http://www.mitre.org/tech/alembic-workbench/
- Apple Pie Parser:
  http://nlp.cs.nyu.edu/app/
- Babel
  http://www.cl.uni-bremen.de/~stefan/Babel/
- Brill Tagger
  http://www.cs.jhu.edu/~brill/
- CLAWS
  http://ucrel.lancs.ac.uk/claws
- SCOL
  http://www.research.att.com/~abney/
- CtxMatch
  http://dit.unitn.it/~zanobini/
- Fastr
  http://www.limsi.fr/Individu/jacquemi/FASTR/
- Gate
  http://gate.ac.uk/
- Java WordNet Library (JWNL)
  http://sourceforge.net/projects/jwordnet
- Connexor Machinese
  http://www.connexor.com/
- MXPOSR Tagger
  http://www.cis.upenn.edu/~adwait/statnlp.html
- Heart of Gold
  http://heartofgold.dfki.de/
- QTag
  http://www.english.bham.ac.uk/staff/omason/software/qtag.html

- Sleepy Student Parser
  `http://www.coli.uni-saarland.de/~adubey/sleepy/`
- Stanford Lexicalized Parser
  `http://nlp.stanford.edu/downloads/lex-parser.shtml`
- Trainable Information Extractor (TIE)
  `http://www.inf.fu-berlin.de/inst/ag-db/software/ties/`
- TiMBL Tagger
  `http://ilk.uvt.nl/timbl/`
- Trigrams'n'Tags (TnT)
  `http://www.coli.uni-saarland.de/~thorsten/tnt/`
- TreeTagger
  `http://www.ims.uni-stuttgart.de/projekte/corplex/TreeTagger/`
- Xerox XRCE Tagger
  `http://www.xrce.xerox.com/competencies/content-analysis/fsnlp/`
  `tagger.en.html`

D.2 Parsers

- Babel (German)
  `http://hpsg.fu-berlin.de/~stefan/Babel`
- Link Grammar (English)
  `http://www.link.cs.cmu.edu/link`
- Connexor Machinese (multiple languages)
  `http://www.connexor.eu/technology/machinese`
- Infogistics (English)
  `http://www.infogistics.com/`
- INRIA (French)
  `http://alpage.inria.fr/perl/parser.pl`
- LoPar (English & German)
  `http://www.ims.uni-stuttgart.de/tcl/SOFTWARE/LoPar.html`
- Stanford Parser (English)
  `http://nlp.stanford.edu:8080/parser`
- VISL (French)
  `http://visl.sdu.dk/visl/fr/parsing/automatic`

E

Probabilistic IR Model

E.1 Probability Theory

To make this section self-containing, we are going to start with a short summary of some properties within probability theory. An event A is an assertion (or proposition) about the result of an experiment, and $P(A)$ is the probability that an event happens with $0 \leq P(A) \leq 1$. E.g., $A =$ "throwing a 6 with a dice", then $P(A) = \frac{1}{6}$. Furthermore, $\overline{A}$ is the complement of A, and:

$$P(\overline{A}) = 1 - P(A). \tag{E.1}$$

The probability that several independent events will occur is known as the *Naive Bayes conditional independence assumption* and is written:

$$P(A_1 \cap A_2 \cap ... \cap A_n) = \prod_{i=1}^{n} P(A_i). \tag{E.2}$$

Let A and B be two independent events, and suppose that event B happened. What is now the probability that A will happen, knowing that B has already occurred?

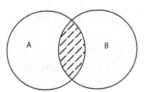

This conditional relationship between A and B is written:

$$P(A \cap B) = P(A|B) \cdot P(B).$$

Also:

$$P(A|B) \cdot P(B) = P(B|A) \cdot P(A),$$

which leads to the *Bayes formula*:

$$P(A|B) = \frac{P(B|A) \cdot P(A)}{P(B)}. \tag{E.3}$$

E.2 Probabilistic Model

In the probabilistic IR model, one sets $P(R|\vec{d_j})$ as being the probability that a retrieved document d_j is also in the set of relevant documents R. The similarity of a document d_j to a query q is expressed by the ratio:

$$sim(q, d_j) = \frac{P(R|\vec{d_j})}{P(\overline{R}|\vec{d_j})}.$$

Using Bayes formula in (E.3), we get:

$$sim(q, d_j) = \frac{\frac{P(\vec{d_j}|R) \cdot P(R)}{P(\vec{d_j})}}{\frac{P(\vec{d_j}|\overline{R} \cdot P(\overline{R})}{P(\vec{d_j})}}$$

$$= \frac{P(\vec{d_j}|R) \cdot P(R)}{P(\vec{d_j})} \cdot \frac{P(\vec{d_j})}{P(\vec{d_j}|\overline{R} \cdot P(\overline{R})}$$

$$sim(q, d_j) = \frac{P(R)}{P(\overline{R})} \cdot \frac{P(\vec{d_j}|R)}{P(\vec{d_j}|\overline{R})}$$

Here, $\frac{P(R)}{P(\overline{R})}$ is constant for a given query.

By assuming that the presence or absence of index words in a document are mutually independent, we can apply the *Naive Bayes conditional independence assumption*, as defined in (E.2). This means, that we calculate the probability that all index terms k_i are present in the document d_j.

$$sim(q, d_j) = \frac{P(R)}{P(\overline{R})} \cdot \prod_{i=1}^{n} \frac{P(k_i|R)}{P(k_i|\overline{R})}$$

In the probabilistic model, all index terms are binary, i.e., they are present or absent. Therefore, we can split the formula in:

$$sim(q, d_j) = \frac{P(R)}{P(\overline{R})} \cdot \prod_{i:k_i=1} \frac{P(k_i = 1|R)}{P(k_i = 1|\overline{R})} \cdot \prod_{i:k_i=0} \frac{P(k_i = 0|R)}{P(k_i = 0|\overline{R})}$$

Here, $P(k_i = 0|R)$ stands for the probability that the index term k_i is absent in a document randomly selected from the set R, and $P(k_i = 1|R)$

stands for the probability that the index term k_i is present in a document randomly selected from the set R.

By assuming that index terms which do not occur in the query ($k_i = 0$) are equally likely to occur in relevant (R) and non-relevant ($\overline{R}$) documents, we can apply the formula defined in (E.1), and simplify the previous result as follows:

$$sim(q, d_j) = \frac{P(R)}{P(\overline{R})} \cdot \prod_{i:k_i=q_i=1} \frac{P(k_i|R)}{P(k_i|\overline{R})} \cdot \prod_{i:k_i=0,q_i=1} \frac{1 - P(k_i|R)}{1 - P(k_i|\overline{R})}$$

Here, the left-hand product is about query terms found in the document, and the right-hand product is about query terms not found in the document. To include all query terms in the right-hand product we can write:

$$sim(q, d_j) = \frac{P(R)}{P(\overline{R})} \cdot \prod_{i:k_i=q_i=1} \frac{P(k_i|R)}{P(k_i|\overline{R})} \cdot \prod_{i:k_i=q_i=1} \frac{1 - P(k_i|\overline{R})}{1 - P(k_i|R)} \cdot$$

$$\prod_{i:k_i=0,q_i=1} \frac{1 - P(k_i|R)}{1 - P(k_i|\overline{R})} \cdot \prod_{i:k_i=q_i=1} \frac{1 - P(k_i|R)}{1 - P(k_i|\overline{R})}$$

$$sim(q, d_j) = \frac{P(R)}{P(\overline{R})} \cdot \prod_{i:k_i=q_i=1} \frac{P(k_i|R) \cdot (1 - P(k_i|\overline{R}))}{P(k_i|\overline{R}) \cdot (1 - P(k_i|R))} \cdot \prod_{i:q_i=1} \frac{1 - P(k_i|R)}{1 - P(k_i|\overline{R})}$$

The advantage of this writing is that the right-hand product is over all query terms (present or absent) in a document, and is therefore constant for a given query. Finally, the only quantity that needs to be computed is the left-hand product.

Terms that occur very often are semantically less important (see section 5.2.2). Therefore, the weight of terms is generally expressed on a logarithmic scale, and written:

$$sim(q, d_j) = \frac{P(R)}{P(\overline{R})} \cdot \prod_{i:q_i=1} \frac{1 - P(k_i|R)}{1 - P(k_i|\overline{R})} \cdot log \prod_{i:k_i=q_i=1} \frac{P(k_i|R) \cdot (1 - P(k_i|\overline{R}))}{P(k_i|\overline{R}) \cdot (1 - P(k_i|R))}$$

$$= \frac{P(R)}{P(\overline{R})} \cdot \prod_{i:q_i=1} \frac{1 - P(k_i|R)}{1 - P(k_i|\overline{R})} \cdot \sum_{i:k_i=q_i=1} log \frac{P(k_i|R) \cdot (1 - P(k_i|\overline{R}))}{P(k_i|\overline{R}) \cdot (1 - P(k_i|R))}$$

$$sim(q, d_j) = \frac{P(R)}{P(\overline{R})} \cdot \prod_{i:q_i=1} \frac{1 - P(k_i|R)}{1 - P(k_i|\overline{R})} \cdot$$

$$\sum_{i:k_i=q_i=1} log \frac{P(k_i|R)}{1 - P(k_i|R)} + log \frac{1 - P(k_i|\overline{R})}{P(k_i|\overline{R})}$$

As only the sum is variable for each document, we can simplify the expression as follows:

$$sim(q, d_j) \approx \sum_{i=1}^{n} log \frac{P(k_i|R)}{1 - P(k_i|R)} + log \frac{1 - P(k_i|\overline{R})}{P(k_i|\overline{R})} \qquad \text{(E.4)}$$

When the query is initiated, and the retrieval process begins, no initial values for $P(k_i|R)$ and $P(k_i|\overline{R})$ are available. Therefore, they are initialized as follows:

$$P(k_i|R) = 0.5 \qquad\qquad P(k_i|\overline{R}) = \frac{n_i}{N}$$

where N is the total number of documents, and n_i is the number of documents which contain the index term k_i. We assume that each index term has even odds of appearing in a relevant document.

After the retrieval process has started, the ranking of documents is improved in an iterative process. Let V be the subset of retrieved documents so far, and $|V|$ the length of V, i.e., the number of retrieved documents so far. Let V_i be the subset of V composed of documents which contain the index term k_i. Then, the ranking of documents can be computed (without human interaction) as follows:

$$P(k_i|R) = \frac{|V_i| + 0.5}{|V| + 1} \qquad \text{and} \qquad P(k_i|\overline{R}) = \frac{n_i - |V_i| + 0.5}{N - |V| + 1}.$$

The constants 0.5 and 1 are introduced in the above formulas to avoid problems for small sets of documents. The computation of $P(k_i|R)$ and $P(k_i|\overline{R})$ is repeated until the ranking of the returned results converges.

References

[AH08]   Dean Allemang and Jim Hendler. *Semantic Web for the Working On-tologist - Effective Modeling in RDFS and OWL.* Morgan Kaufmann, 2008.

[All94]   James Allen. *Natural Language Understanding.* Addison Wesley, 1994.

[AMO⁺03]   Jürgen Angele, Eddie Mönch, Henrik Oppermann, Steffen Staab, and Dirk Wenke. Ontology-Based Query and Answering in Chemistry: OntoNova @ Project Halo. In *International Semantic Web Conference (ISWC)*, pages 913–928, 2003.

[AvH04]   Grigoris Antoniou and Frank van Harmelen. *A Semantic Web Primer.* MIT Press, 2004.

[BCFB04]   Dario Bonino, Fulvio Corno, Laura Farinetti, and Alessio Bosca. Ontology driven semantic search. *WSEAS Transaction on Information Science and Application,* 1(6):1597–1605, 2004.

[BCM⁺03]   Franz Baader, Diego Calvanese, Deborah L. McGuinness, Daniele Nardi, and Peter F. Patel-Schneider, editors. *The Description Logic Handbook: Theory, Implementation, and Applications.* Cambridge University Press, 2003.

[BCT07]   Karin Breitman, Marco Antonio Casanova, and Walt Truszkowski. *Semantic Web: Concepts, Technologies and Applications.* Springer-Verlag Berlin Heidelberg New York, 2007.

[Ber10]   Mike Bergman. The sweet compendium of ontol-ogy building tools. http://www.mkbergman.com/862/the-sweet-compendium-of-ontology-building-tools/, 2010.

[Bev70]   Thomas G. Bever. *Cognition and the Development of Language,* chapter The Cognitive Basis for Linguistic Structures, page 279362. Wiley, New York, 1970.

[BH06]   Alexander Budanitsky and Graeme Hirst. Evaluating WordNet-based Measures of Lexical Semantic Relatedness. *Computational Linguistics,* 32(1):13–47, 2006.

[BHyP⁺06]   Boualem Benatallah, Mohand-Said Hacid, Hye young Paik, Christophe Rey, and Farouk Toumani. Towards semantic-driven, flex-ible and scalable framework for peering and querying e-catalog com-munities. *Information Systems,* 31(4):266–294, 2006.

[BKM99]   Franz Baader, Ralf Küsters, and Ralf Molitor. Computing Least Common Subsumers in Description Logics with Existential Restrictions.
In *International Joint Conference on Artificial Intelligence (IJCAI)*,
pages 96–101, 1999.

[BKM00]   Franz Baader, Ralph Küsters, and Ralf Molitor. Rewriting Concepts
Using Terminologies. In *Knowledge Representation (KR)*, pages 297–
308, 2000.

[BKT02]   Sebastian Brandt, Ralf Küsters, and Anni-Yasmin Turhan. Approxi-
mation and Difference in Description Logics. In *Knowledge Representation (KR)*, pages 203–214, 2002.

[BLHL01]   Tim Berners-Lee, James Hendler, and Ora Lassila. The Semantic Web.
Scientific American, 284(5):35–43, 2001.

[Blo01]   François-Marie Blondel. La recherche d'informations sur internet par
des lycéens, analyse et assistance à l'apprentissage. In *Hypermédias
et Apprentissages*, pages 119–133, 2001.

[BP98]   Sergey Brin and Larry Page. The Anatomy of a Large-Scale Hyper-
textual Web Search Engine. In *World Wide Web (WWW)*, pages
107–117, 1998.

[Bra06]   Sebastian Brandt. *Standard and Non-Standard Reasoning in Description Logics*. PhD thesis, Technische Universitt Dresden, 2006.

[BVL03]   Sean Bechhofer, Raphael Volz, and Phillip W. Lord. Cooking the
Semantic Web with the OWL API. In *International Semantic Web
Conference (ISWC)*, pages 659–675, 2003.

[BWH05]   Alexander Borgida, Thomas Walsh, and Haym Hirsh. Towards Mea-
suring Similarity in Description Logics. In *Description Logics (DL)*,
2005.

[BYRN99]   Ricardo A. Baeza-Yates and Berthier A. Ribeiro-Neto. *Modern Information Retrieval*. ACM Press / Addison-Wesley, 1999.

[CDD⁺04]   Jeremy J. Carroll, Ian Dickinson, Chris Dollin, Dave Reynolds, Andy
Seaborne, and Kevin Wilkinson. Jena: implementing the semantic web
recommendations. In *World Wide Web (WWW) - Alternate Track
Papers & Posters*, pages 74–83, 2004.

[CEE⁺01]   Kai-Uwe Carstenense, Christian Ebert, Cornelia Endriss, Susanne
Jekat, Ralf Klabunde, and Hagen Langer, editors. *Computerlinguis-
tik und Sprachentechnologie: Eine Einfhrung*. Spektrum Akademsicher
Verlag, Heidelberg-Berlin, 2001.

[CNS⁺03]   Simona Colucci, Tommaso Di Noia, Eugenio Di Sciascio, Francesco M.
Donini, and Marina Mongiello. Concept Abduction and Contraction
in Description Logics. In *Description Logics (DL)*, 2003.

[CNS⁺05]   Simona Colucci, Tommaso Di Noia, Eugenio Di Sciascio, Francesco M.
Donini, and Azzurra Ragone. *The Semantic Web: Research and Applications*, chapter Semantic-Based Automated Composition of Distributed Learning Objects for Personalized E-Learning, pages 633–
648. Springer-Verlag Berlin Heidelberg New York, 2005.

[dFE06]   Claudia d'Amato, Nicola Fanizzi, and Floriana Esposito. A dissimi-
larity measure for ALC concept descriptions. In *ACM SIGSAC*, pages
1695–1699, 2006.

[DuB93]   Michael DuBois. *Readings in Fuzzy Sets for Intelligent Systems*. Morgan Kaufmann Publishers Inc., 1993.

[EHLS06]   Michael Engelhardt, Arne Hildebrand, Dagmar Lange, and Thomas C. Schmidt. Reasoning about eLearning Multimedia Objects. In *Semantic Web Annotations for Multimedia (SWAMM)*, 2006.

[ES07]   Jérôme Euzenat and Pavel Shvaiko. *Ontology matching.* Springer-Verlag Berlin Heidelberg New York, 2007.

[FDD⁺88]   George W. Furnas, Scott C. Deerwester, Susan T. Dumais, Thomas K. Landauer, Richard A. Harshman, Lynn A. Streeter, and Karen E. Lochbaum. Information Retrieval using a Singular Value Decomposition Model of Latent Semantic Structure. In *ACM SIGIR*, pages 465–480, 1988.

[FDD⁺99]   Raya Fidel, Rachel K. Davies, Mary H. Douglass, Jenny K. Holder, Carla J. Hopkins, Elisabeth J. Kushner, Bryan K. Miyagishima, and Christina D. Toney. A Visit to the Information Mall: Web Searching Behavior of High School Students. *American Society for Information Science*, 50(1):24–37, 1999.

[Fen04]   Dieter Fensel. *Ontologies: A Silver Bullet for Knowledge Management and Electronic Commerce.* Springer-Verlag Berlin Heidelberg New York, 2004.

[For73]   David G. Forney. The viterbi algorithm. *IEEE*, 61(3):268–278, 1973.

[Fra03]   Enrico Franconi. *The Description Logic Handbook: Theory, Implementation, and Applications*, chapter Natural Language Processing, pages 450–461. Cambridge University Press, 2003.

[GPCGFL03]   Asuncion Gomez-Perez, Oscar Corcho-Garcia, and Mariano Fernandez-Lopez. *Ontological Engineering.* Springer-Verlag Berlin Heidelberg New York, 2003.

[Gro10]   W3C OWL Working Group. DL Reasoners. WWW page, 2010. http://www.w3.org/2007/OWL/wiki/Implementations.

[Gru93]   Thomas R. Gruber. A translation approach to portable ontologies. *Knowledge Acquisition*, 5(2):199–220, 1993.

[Haf10]   Kimberly A. Haffner, editor. *Semantic Web - Standards, Tools and Ontologies.* Nova, 2010.

[HCG⁺10]   Chu-Ren Huang, Nicoletta Calzolari, Aldo Gangemi, Alessandro Lenci, Allesandro Oltramari, and Laurent Prévot, editors. *Studies in Natural Language Processing - Ontology and the Lexicon.* Cambridge University Press, 2010.

[HdCD⁺05]   Frank W. Hartel, Sherri de Coronado, Robert Dionne, Gilberto Fragoso, and Jennifer Golbeck. Modeling a description logic vocabulary for cancer research. *Biomedical Informatics*, 38:114–129, 2005.

[Hea78]   Harold Stanley Heaps. *Information Retrieval: Computational and Theoretical Aspects.* Academic Press, 1978.

[Hje01]   Johan Hjelm. *Creating the Semantic Web with RDF: Professional Developer's Guide.* John Wiley & Sons, 2001.

[HKR10]   Pascal Hitzler, Markus Krötzsch, and Sebastian Rudolph. *Foundations of Semantic Web Technologies.* CRC Press, 2010.

[HLRT02]   Mohand-Sad Hacid, Alain Leger, Christophe Rey, and Farouk Toumani. Computing concept covers: A preliminary report. In *Description Logics (DL)*, 2002.

[HM01]   Volker Haarslev and Ralf Möller. Racer system description. In *International Joint Conference on Automated Reasoning (IJCAR)*, pages 701–706, 2001.

[HM02]   Elliotte Rusty Harold and W. Scott Means. *XML in a Nutshell, 2nd Edition.* O'Reilly, 2002.

[HPM05]   Andreas Holzinger, Arnold Pichler, and Hermann Maurer. Multi Media e-Learning Software TRIANGLE Case-Study: Experimental Results and Lessons Learned. *Universal Science and Technology of Learning*, 0(0):61–92, 2005.

[HS00]   Christoph Hölscher and Gerhard Strube. Web search behavior of Internet experts and newbies. *Computer Networks*, 33(1-6):337–346, 2000.

[Inm04]   Dave Inman. *The possibility of Natural Language Processing by computer.* `http://www.scism.sbu.ac.uk/inmandw/tutorials/nlp/intro/intro.html`, 2004.

[KEW01]   Cody C. T. Kwok, Oren Etzioni, and Daniel S. Weld. Scaling question answering to the web. In *World Wide Web (WWW)*, pages 150–161, 2001.

[KF60]   Henry Kucera and W. Nelson Francis. *Brown Corpus Manual.* Brown University, 1960.

[KFNM04]   Holger Knublauch, Ray W. Fergerson, Natalya Fridman Noy, and Mark A. Musen. The Protégé OWL Plugin: An Open Development Environment for Semantic Web Applications. In *International Semantic Web Conference (ISWC)*, pages 229–243, 2004.

[KK01]   Barbara Krasner-Khait. Survivor: The History of the Library. *History Magazine*, 2001.

[KLM07]   Naouel Karam, Serge Linckels, and Christoph Meinel. Semantic Composition of Lecture Subparts for a Personalized e-Learning. In *European Semantic Web Conference (ESWC)*, pages 716–728, 2007.

[Kos94]   Martijn Koster. Aliweb - Archie-Like Indexing in the Web. In *World Wide Web (WWW)*, pages 175–182, 1994.

[KS05]   Dimitris J. Kavvadias and Elias C. Stavropoulos. An Efficient Algorithm for the Transversal Hypergraph Generation. *Graph Algorithms Applications*, 9(2):239–264, 2005.

[Küs01]   Ralf Küsters. *Non-Standard Inferences in Description Logics.* Springer-Verlag Berlin Heidelberg New York, 2001.

[Lac05]   Lee W. Lacy. *OWL: Representing Information Using the Web Ontology Language.* Trafford Publishing, 2005.

[LDM06]   Serge Linckels, Carole Dording, and Christoph Meinel. Better Results in Mathematics Lessons with a Virtual Personal Teacher. In *ACM SIGUCCS*, pages 201–209, 2006.

[Lev66]   Vladimir Levenshtein. Binary Codes Capable of Correcting Deletions, Insertions and Reversals. *Soviet Physics Doklady*, 10, 1966.

[LM01]   Ora Lassila and Deborah McGuinness. The Role of Frame-Based Representation on the Semantic Web. *Electronic transactions on Artificial Intelligence (ETAI)*, 2001.

[LM07]   Serge Linckels and Christoph Meinel. Semantic Interpretation of Natural Language User Input to Improve Search in Multimedia Knowledge Base. *it - Information Technology*, 1(49):40–48, 2007.

[LTV03]   Ulrike Lucke, Djamshid Tavangarian, and Denny Voigt. Multidimensional Educational Multimedia with $<ML>^3$. In *E-Learning in Corporate, Government, Healthcare, and Higher Education (ELEARN)*, 2003.

[Ma98]   George A. Miller and al. *WordNet: An Electronic Lexical Database.*
            The MIT Press, 1998.
[MBR01]   Jayant Madhavan, Philip A. Bernstein, and Erhard Rahm. Generic
            Schema Matching with Cupid. In *Very Large Databases (VLDB)*,
            pages 49–58, 2001.
[Mit04]   Ruslan Mitkov, editor. *The Oxford Handbook of Computational Lin-
            guistics.* Oxford University Press, 2004.
[MRS08]   Christopher D. Manning, Prabhakar Raghavan, and Hinrich Schütze.
            Introduction to Information Retrieval. Cambridge University Press,
            2008.
[MS99]   Christopher D. Manning and Hinrich Schtze. *Foundations of Statisti-
            cal Natural Language Processing.* The MIT Press, 1999.
[MS04]   Christoph Meinel and Harald Sack. *WWW - Kommunikation, In-
            ternetworking, Web-Technologien.* Springer-Verlag Berlin Heidelberg
            New York, 2004.
[MS09]   Christoph Meinel and Harald Sack. *Digitale Kommunikation.*
            Springer-Verlag Berlin Heidelberg New York, 2009.
[MS11a]   Christoph Meinel and Harald Sack. *Internetworking.* Springer-Verlag
            Berlin Heidelberg New York, 2011.
[MS11b]   Christoph Meinel and Harald Sack. *Web-Technologien.* Springer-
            Verlag Berlin Heidelberg New York, 2011.
[Neb90]   Bernhard Nebel. *Reasoning and revision in hybrid representation sys-
            tems.* Springer-Verlag Berlin Heidelberg New York, 1990.
[NSDM03]   Tommaso Di Noia, Eugenio Di Sciascio, Francesco M. Donini, and
            Marina Mongiello. Abductive Matchmaking using Description Logics.
            In *International Joint Conference on Artificial Intelligence (IJCAI)*,
            pages 337–342, 2003.
[PB06]   Tassilio Pellegrini and Andreas Blumauer, editors. *Semantic Web
            - Wege zu vernetzten Wissensgesellschaft.* X.media.press, Springer-
            Verlag Berlin Heidelberg New York, 2006.
[PBR06]   Jane C. Prey, Dave Berque, and Robert H. Reed. *The Impact of Tablet
            PCs and Pen-based Technology on Education: Vignettes, Evaluations,
            and Future Directions.* Purdue University Press, 2006.
[Pea88]   Judea Pearl. *Probabilistic Reasoning in Intelligent Systems:Networks
            of Plausible Inference.* Morgan Kaufmann, 1988.
[Pop05]   Octav Popescu. *Logic-Based Natural Language Understanding in In-
            telligent Tutoring Systems.* PhD thesis, Carnegie Mellon University,
            2005.
[Pow03]   Shelley Powers. *Practical RDF. Solving Problems with the Resource
            Description Framework.* O'Reilly Media, 2003.
[RDH+04]   Alan L. Rector, Nick Drummond, Matthew Horridge, Jeremy Rogers,
            Holger Knublauch, Robert Stevens, Hai Wang, and Chris Wroe. OWL
            Pizzas: Practical Experience of Teaching OWL-DL: Common Errors
            & Common Patterns. In *Engineering Knowledge in the Age of the
            Semantic Web (EKAW)*, pages 63–81, 2004.
[Rep09]   Stephan Repp. *Extraktion von semantischen Informationen aus au-
            diovisuellen Vorlesungsaufzeichnungen.* PhD thesis, Hasso-Plattner-
            Institut (HPI), University of Potsdam, 2009.

[RM06]   Stephan Repp and Christoph Meinel. Semantic Indexing for Recorded
              Educational Lecture Videos. In *International Conference on Pervasive
              Computing and Communications Workshops (PERCOMW)*, page 240,
              2006.

[RNM96]   Berthier A. Ribeiro-Neto and Richard R. Muntz. A Belief Network
              Model for IR. In *ACM SIGIR*, pages 253–260, 1996.

[SBPK06]   Tobias Sager, Abraham Bernstein, Martin Pinzger, and Christoph
              Kiefer. Detecting Similar Java Classes Using Tree Algorithms. In
              International Workshop on Mining Software Repositories, pages 65–
              71, Shanghai, China, 2006.

[Sch93]   Renate A. Schmidt. Terminological Representation, Natural Language
              & Relation Algebra. In *German AI Conference (GWAI)*, pages 357–
              371, 1993.

[SF99]   Christian Süß and Burkhard Freitag. Metamodeling for Web-Based
              Teachware Management. In *Advances in Conceptual Modeling*, pages
              360–373, 1999.

[SFW83]   Gerard Salton, Edward A. Fox, and Harry Wu. Extended Boolean
              Information Retrieval. *Communications of the ACM*, 26(11):1022–
              1036, 1983.

[SP04]   Evren Sirin and Bijan Parsia. Pellet: An OWL DL reasoner. In *De-
              scription Logics (DL)*, 2004.

[SS04]   Steffen Staab and Rudi Studer, editors. *Handbook on Ontologies*. Inter-
              national Handbooks on Information Systems. Springer-Verlag Berlin
              Heidelberg New York, 2004.

[SSS91]   Manfred Schmidt-Schauß and Gert Smolka. Attributive Concept De-
              scriptions with Complements. *Artificial Intelligence*, 48(1):1–26, 1991.

[Stu09]   Heiner Stuckenschmidt. *Ontologien - Konzepte, Technologien und An-
              wendungen*. Springer-Verlag Berlin Heidelberg New York, 2009.

[Tee94]   Gunnar Teege. Making the difference: a subtraction operation for
              description logics. In *Knowledge Representation (KR)*, pages 540–550,
              1994.

[TGF⁺07]   Javier Tejedor, Roberto Garca, Miriam Fernndez, Fernando J. Lpez-
              Colino, Ferrn Perdrix, Jos A. Macas, Rosa M. Gil, Marta Oliva, Diego
              Moya, Jos Cols, and Pablo Castells. Ontology-Based Retrieval of Hu-
              man Speech. In *Web Semantics (WebS)*, 2007.

[Vel10]   Yannis Velegrakis. *Semantic Web Information Management - A
              Model-Based Perspective*, chapter Relational Technologies, Metadata
              and RDF, pages 41 – 66. Springer-Verlag Berlin Heidelberg New York,
              2010.

[W3C10]   W3C. Linked Data. `http://www.w3.org/standards/semanticweb/`
              `data`, 2010.

[WAC84]   Robert Wilensky, Yigal Arens, and David Chin. Talking to UNIX in
              English: an overview of UC. *Communications of the ACM*, 27(6):574–
              593, 1984.

[WH91]   Ross Wilkinson and Philip Hingston. Using the cosine measure in a
              neural network for document retrieval. In *ACM SIGIR*, pages 202–210,
              1991.

[WLM07]   Katrin Wolf, Serge Linckels, and Christoph Meinel. Teleteaching Any-
              where Solution Kit (tele-TASK) Goes Mobile. In *ACM SIGUCCS*,
              pages 366–371, 2007.

[WZW85]   S. K. Michael Wong, Wojciech Ziarko, and P. C. N. Wong. Generalized Vector Space Model in Information Retrieval. In *ACM SIGIR*, pages 18–25, 1985.

[Zip49]   George Zipf.   *Human Behavior and the Principle of Least Effort.* Addison-Wesley, 1949.

Index